DROITWICH

D1586327

Please return/renew this item by the last date shown

worcestershire
countycouncil
Libraries & Learning

# DARK PEAK HIKES
# Off the Beaten Track

## Doug Brown

1st Edition 2006

Published by Sigma Leisure – an imprint of Sigma Press, Stobart House, Pontyclerc, Penybanc Road, Ammanford, Carms SA18 3HP, Wales

British Library Cataloguing in Publication Data
A CIP record for this book is available from the British Library.

ISBN: 1-85058-883-2

Typesetting and Design by: Sigma Press, Ammanford, Carms

Cover photograph: Mountain hare footprints in the snow by the Wainstones on Bleaklowby (Doug Brown)

Maps and photographs: Doug Brown

Printed by: Berforts Group Limited

Disclaimer: the information in this book is given in good faith and is believed to be correct at the time of publication. No responsibility is accepted by either the author or publisher for errors or omissions, or for any loss or injury howsoever caused. Only you can judge your own fitness, competence and experience. Do not rely solely on sketch maps for navigation: we strongly recommend the use of appropriate Ordnance Survey (or equivalent) maps.

# Preface

This book contains a selection of walks in the Dark Peak District, situated at the southern end of the Pennines. The walks explore areas away from the main paths. They are designed for people who enjoy the challenge of wandering off the beaten track and using their navigational skills for route finding and locating items of interest. Many map references are given to help navigation over open moorland in poor visibility.

Interesting features include aircraft wrecks, memorials, a bothy, Bronze Age barrows, Iron Age forts, industrial heritage and even a mysterious marker planted by the Aetherius Society.

Most of the walks are between 10km and 20km. They require a reasonable level of fitness and experience. On a clear day, the Dark Peak provides some lovely walks with wide-ranging views. In adverse conditions, walking and route finding can be a real challenge.

Although many areas covered by the walks in this book have been open to the public for a long time, the recent 'right to roam' act has made some new parts of the district open access. Patrick Monkhouse's book On Foot in the Peak, first published in 1932, gives a picture of how different it was in the 1930s. It also shows the great debt we owe to all those people who have worked so hard over the intervening years to improve the situation to what it is today. In a way this book is a tribute to these people and celebrates our right to roam. Wandering freely over the moors without having to worry about rights of way leads to a much more relaxed state of mind, enabling one to enjoy the space and superb scenery.

The walks are arranged into five main sections:
1. Kinder Scout – south of the Snake Pass
2. Bleaklow – between Snake Pass and Woodhead Pass
3. Black Hill – between Woodhead Pass and the A635
4. Eastern Moors – Margery Hill, Stanage and Bamford Edges
5. Others – outside the above areas, and two longer walks

I include one walk around Combs Moss, which is on the White Peak District map. The rock is gritstone and the terrain is similar to that of the

Dark Peak. Also, it is part of a map-reading/orienteering course designed by the climber Joe Brown, and this is described in Walks 27 and 33.

Doug Brown

# Contents

## Introduction

## *The Walks*

### Section 1: Kinder Scout

## Section 2: Bleaklow

## Section 3: Black Hill

# Section 4: The Eastern Moors

# Section 5: Other Walks

# Further suggestions

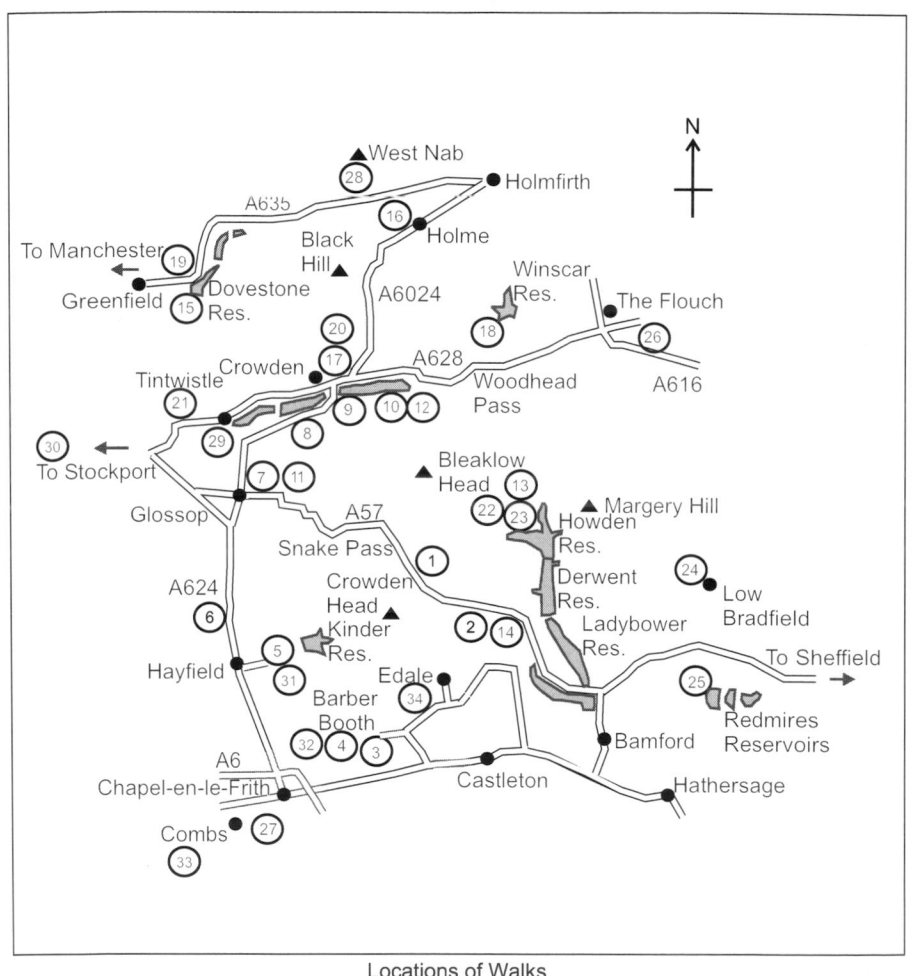

Locations of Walks

# Introduction

## An early experience

My first walk in the Dark Peak District was a few decades ago. A friend, Paul, suggested that we pay a visit to Kinder. His son, Alex came with us. The snow started falling shortly after we left Hayfield. By the time we had reached Kinder Downfall the snow made it impossible to see more than a few feet in front of us. We crossed the plateau to Fair Brook. The snow and wind made the conditions on top extremely unpleasant so we decided to return across the ground below Ashop Edge. The snow was deep, particularly at the bottom of the cloughs that come down from the Edge. Floundering around, at times up to our waists or above, it took us hours to get back. We were exhausted by the time we reached the safety of the road. However, we did have a few laughs at our predicament. This was a fine introduction to the area.

## Access

The recent changes have increased the amount of land that is open access. However, there can be the occasional problem reaching this land. I have tried to give clear directions how this can be achieved. It is worth checking routes, as there may be changes or additions to the access points.

Many of the walks involve open moorland. It is advisable to avoid doing these during the nesting season. Also, from August 12th, the start of the grouse-shooting season, sections of the moors may be closed on certain days. Landowners do not allow dogs on some moors, even though they are open access land.

## Distances and times

The routes may involve negotiating over boggy ground, heather moors and include some easy scrambling. I find that a speed of 3km/h (2mph) or less is to be expected over this type of terrain. It is easy to underestimate the time required. The times given are rough guidelines. A fast party in good conditions may take less than the minimum times suggested. However in very poor conditions, requiring frequent stops for checking navigation and rests, it can take a lot longer than expected to cover what may appear to be a short distance.

## Grades

Although most of these walks are not long, the terrain is often difficult. If walkers are unsure as to the nature of these types of walks they should try one of the easy ones to start with.

## Parking

I have tried to start walks from places that have good car parking. Also, most of these points are on public transport routes.

## Scrambles

Many of the stream beds and cloughs provide entertaining scrambles. Most of these can be easily avoided where they are difficult or if conditions are poor, but they do add variety to a walk. It is possible to choose routes that require balance and skill. I have tried to indicate some of their more interesting parts.

## Maps

The maps are only rough sketches. 1: 25 000 Ordnance Survey maps are essential and should be referred to when planning a walk. The Peak District OL1 Explorer map covers all but one of the walks. The exception is the walk round Combs Moss for which map OL24 is required.

## Map references

Where precise data is required, a 10-figure reference is given as well the 6-figure reference. In particular, this helps the walker who has a GPS. A 6-figure reference indicates a point in a 100 metre square grid. A 10-figure reference implies accuracy to 1 metre, which is unrealistic. However, it is usually accurate to within 10 metres.

To get the 6-figure reference from a 10-figure reference simply take the first three figures from each half. For example: 01234/56789 becomes 012567. I have not attempted to round the figures as that might lead to unnecessary confusion.

## Global Positioning System (GPS)

Many walkers now own a GPS. The ability to use a map and compass is essential but there are occasions, in poor conditions, when it is easy to become unsure of one's exact location. A basic GPS can give a very precise map reference. Also, looking for a particular point, such as a small amount of aircraft wreckage, when in mist or cloud can be difficult and time consuming. My own experience, so far, is that the data given is very reliable. I tend to use my GPS only when I think I might have made a mistake or to locate a particular spot precisely.

## Navigation

These walks are designed for experienced walkers who are competent with a compass and at map reading. In cloudy conditions the Peak District requires good navigational skills. It is difficult to keep on a straight line when wandering through a maze of groughs. The moors are often featureless. Fortunately the Kinder plateau is relatively small so it isn't too difficult to get off it. However, there are a few cliff edges that can be dangerous in very poor visibility. Some parts of Bleaklow and Black Hill are more extensive and becoming lost can be a serious matter.

From my own experience I know how easy it is to get lost. A couple of years ago, on the Marsden to Edale Walk, in daylight, we missed Grindsbrook and came down Crowden Brook. Our navigator came in for considerable criticism and felt compelled to run ahead to The Rambler to buy placating refreshments. More recently a group of friends set off from the Snake Inn and climbed up to Kinder, wandered around the plateau and found themselves heading down William Clough in the direction of Hayfield. They had intended to return to the Snake Inn. They ended up in the Sportsman, just outside Hayfield, ordered drinks and a taxi for the expensive trip back to the Snake Inn.

## Equipment

All the obvious plus gaiters, which stop all sorts of nasty things getting into your boots, and walking poles – useful for balance, crossing streams and probing boggy ground. Also, a sense of humour is extremely helpful!

## Wildlife

Various species of birds live on the higher ground. Depending on the time of year, these include: snipe, golden plovers, lapwings, curlew, short-eared owls, dunlin, ring ouzels, wheatears, skylarks, meadow pipits, dippers, kestrels, goshawks, peregrines, sparrow-hawks and merlins. The area is also populated by mountain or blue hares. These seem to be increasing in numbers. In summer, I seldom used to see any, but now I find it unusual to see none at all. Some moors seem to support more of them than others. The sharp-eyed walker will spot the occasional lizard. To give an idea of what may be seen, I have mentioned some of the wildlife I have encountered on the walks.

## Aircraft wrecks

On some of the walks the route goes to the sites of aircraft wreckage. During WWII the lack of radar caused many aircraft to crash in poor visibility on high ground. Due to the slower speeds of that time, and the terrain, quite a few airmen survived.

Many of the sites have plaques commemorating those who died. I feel that it is fitting that more people should become aware of these aircrew who sacrificed their lives. Please respect these sites and do not remove any of the wreckage.

Apart from the information in the walk descriptions, there is an appendix at the back of the book that covers most of the wrecks in the Dark Peak.

## Acknowledgements

Thanks to all those friends who have walked and talked the hills with me. They include: Pete Booth, Jan Gage, Robin Fletcher, Chris Hill, Bob Harrison, Tony Hoyland, Brian Jones, Peter Jones, Malcolm Keats, Willie Lees, Tony Lyth, Mike Monaghan, Frank Murphy, Phil Reid, Dave Richardson and Brian Rowntree. I would like to remember two friends who died recently: Paul Barlow and Peter Tarbatt.

# Section 1: Kinder Scout

The highest point of the Kinder Scout plateau is 2088ft or 636m above sea level. This is the highest point in Derbyshire. There are many deep peat groughs in the centre of the plateau. The main features are the Kinder Downfall, the River Kinder, and the oddly shaped rocks on the edge of the plateau.

Trying to walk across the plateau in a straight line isn't easy. A path goes round its edge that, due to the amount of use it receives, can be very muddy. The Pennine Way either crosses the plateau, or keeps to the edge, depending on how difficult you want to make it. There is a well-used path round the head of the Edale valley from Kinder Low, over Brown Knoll to Mam Tor. The most popular ways onto the plateau are from Edale by Grindsbrook, by Jacob's Ladder and from Hayfield by William Clough. There are good paths up Kinderlow End and several more from the Edale valley, including one up to Ringing Roger.

The routes described are mainly along the lesser-used paths and invite the walker to explore the heart of the plateau. Crowden Head is approached from various directions. On a clear day this is not too difficult. However when visibility is poor, even though the plateau does not cover a great area, navigation can be a problem. Two routes start from Barber Booth, two from near Hayfield and two from the Snake Pass.

Note: all the map references in this section lie in an area with the prefix SK.

# Walk 1. Crowden Head and Fair Brook

**Grade:** Easy

**Distance:** 10km (6 miles)

**Time:** 4-5 hours

**Starting point/parking:** One of three lay-bys on the A57 near the Snake Inn, (113905)

## General description

The ascent on to the Kinder plateau is by Fair Brook. There is a good path on the north side of the clough, or the stream bed may be used. The route goes from the edge of the plateau to Crowden Head. (I think of Crowden Head as being the Holy Grail of Kinder. In poor visibility it can be very elusive.) The route returns to the edge near Seal Stones. Alternative ways down are described.

## Route

On the opposite side of the road to the Snake Inn, climb a stile into a wood. A path goes through the wood to a footbridge over the River Ashop. This is 500m from the Snake Inn. Turn left over the bridge, then right, up Fair Brook. Follow the path by the stream until it is possible to use the stream bed. Depending on how much water is flowing down, it may be possible to start using it, just past a pool where the path comes close to the water (104897). This is 1km from the start of the brook. You may get wet feet but there are no other difficulties. Higher up the water flow lessens. Continue up the bed until the plateau is reached (1).

At the top the main clough goes south. A path has been formed along it. On one occasion a wren kept just in front of me for some distance, making its scolding noise. For about 500m the clough leads towards Crowden Head. However, although it is only a further 500m to the cairn at Crowden Head, it is easy to miss it. This last stretch needs good navigation in poor visibility. The map reference of Crowden Head is 095881 (09570/88100). Its height is 2073ft (632m) (2).

From Crowden Head go north for 200m. Then curve to the east, trying to stay on the higher ground above the groughs. There is a rather neat, little cairn at 098885 (09869/88585). You should pass close to it. It is

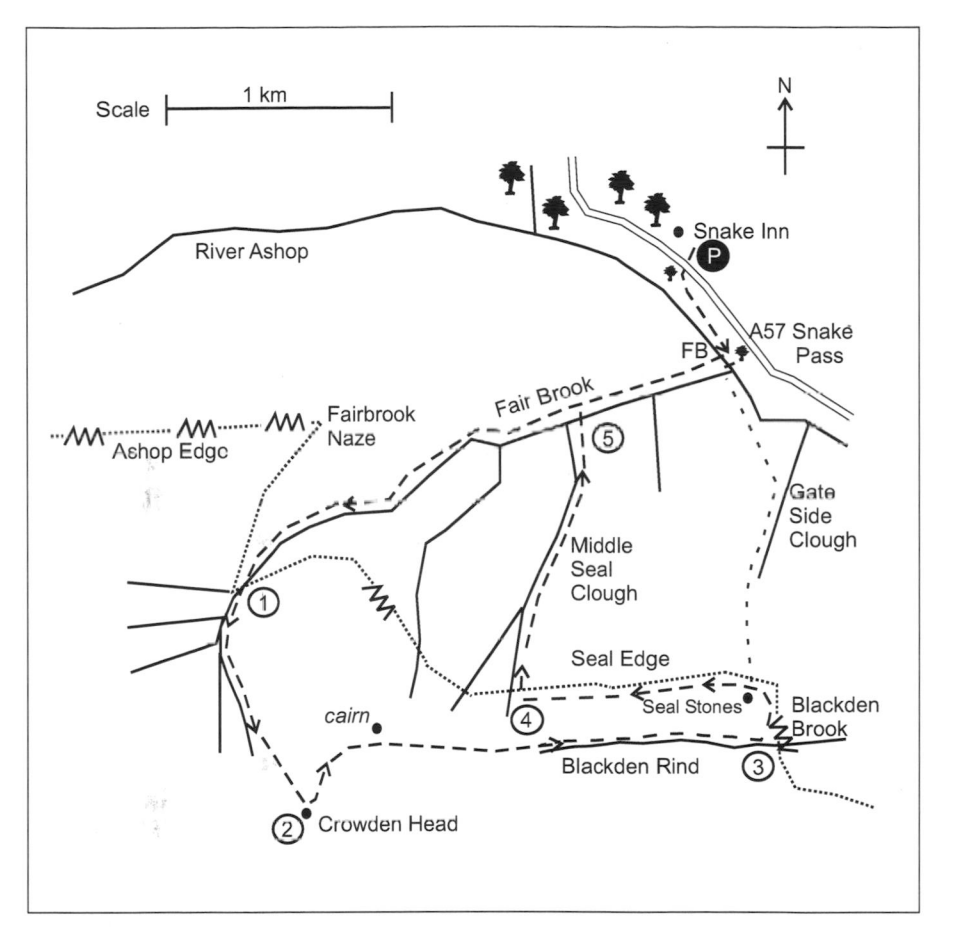

400m from Seal Edge and stands on high ground. The route is close to the northern edge of the plateau, but try to keep heading east. This direction leads into groughs that feed into Blackden Grind and along to the top of Blackden Brook (3). From here, go north along the main path to Seal Stones. The path turns west along Seal Edge. There are fine views to the north.

The first possibility for a way off the edge is by Gate Side Clough. The path starts at 114888 and goes down by a line of grouse butts. It then angles across the steep slope to the bottom of Fair Brook, which has to be crossed to regain the path back towards the Snake Inn.

The suggested route is to go west along Seal Edge for 1km and

Fair Brook grough

descend by Middle Seal Clough (104887) (4). Look for a clough, by rocks, which starts at the edge of the plateau, and is seen descending to the north. Follow the ground by the side of the clough. It starts steeply, then soon levels off. There isn't a path, but you can walk alongside the clough. The ground is boggy in places. A steep bank descends to where the clough meets Fair Brook (5). This is a nice spot to stop for a rest. On the other side of Fair Brook there is a short climb up to the path you started out on. Follow this back to the Snake Pass.

Another alternative, is to enjoy the views from the edge by walking back to the top of Fair Brook and descending by the brook.

# Walk 2. Eastern Kinder and Blackden Brook

**Grade:** Easy

**Distance:** 10km (6 miles)

**Time:** 4-5 hours

**Starting point/parking:** By side of the A57, 2km (1.5 miles) east of the Snake Inn, opposite Blackden View Farm (130895)

## General description

The ascent onto the Kinder plateau is from the Snake Road opposite Blackden View Farm. The route goes up a lovely stream, Blackden Brook, with a choice between easy scrambling and a path. It involves crossing the groughs on the top to reach the southern edge of the plateau. The plateau is re-crossed further to the east. The groughs are not too deep here but can be muddy. Searching for aircraft wrecks provides a chance to practise navigational skills.

## Route

By the parking spot there is a stile and a path that leads down to a bridge over the River Ashop. A word of warning: my old car was broken into when left in this parking place. I made the mistake of leaving an old anorak on the back seat.

Cross the bridge and go straight ahead for 100m, towards a wall. Take the path on the left (east) side of the wall and follow it along the wall. The path goes above Blackden Barn and leads to Blackden Brook. Shortly there is small waterfall that can be climbed on the left side. It is possible to take a path for the whole of the ascent but it is more fun to use the stream bed as soon as possible. It has flat, sloping rocks, some of which are comprised of crumbly slate. Usually there is a good flow of water. It is an attractive brook with some silver birches on its banks. On two occasions I have seen kestrels over the brook. Another time, I saw a dipper fly down the stream.

About 1.5km from the start of the stream there is a 20ft waterfall (121883). The lower part is too slimy to risk trying to climb. However, the

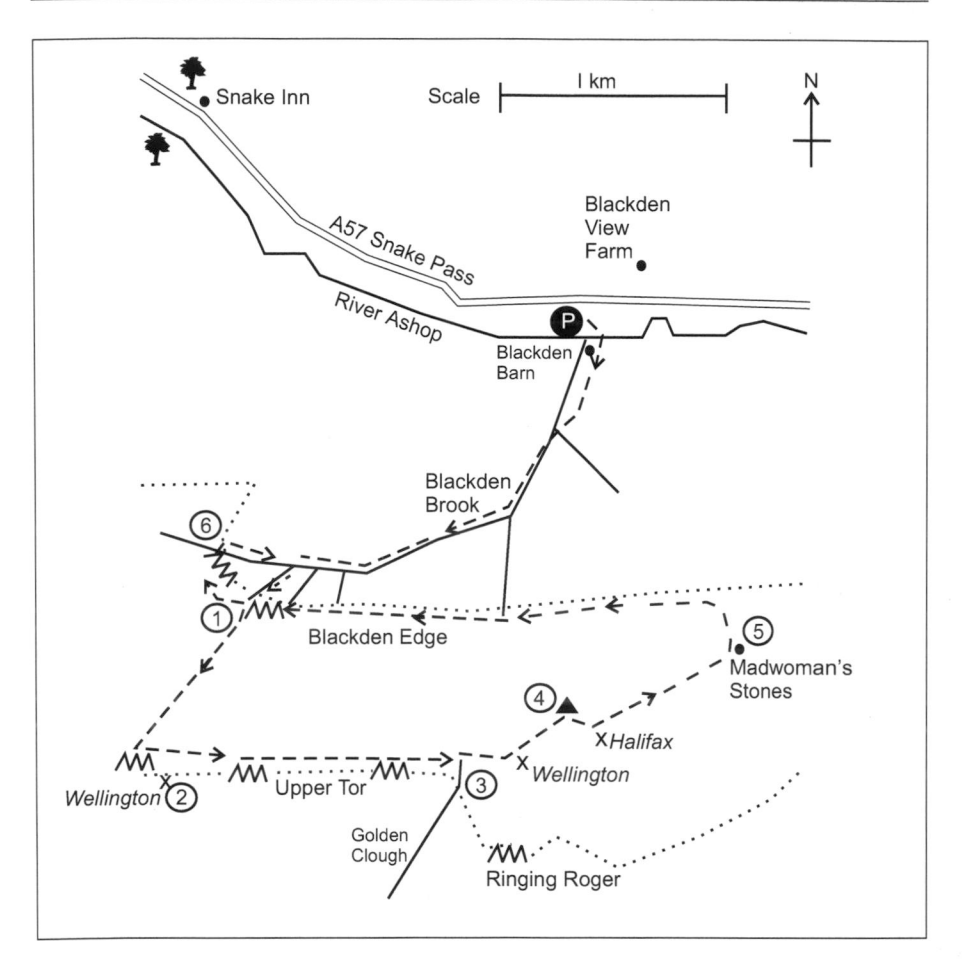

two trees to the right provide a route to scramble up: otherwise use the path. Further on, there are several more small waterfalls that can be climbed. As you near the top, at 117883, there is the first of two gulleys that branch off left from the main gulley. These are 40m apart. Ignore the first; the direct route is too difficult. I have tried it, but decided that the final wall was beyond the level of scrambling. I did manage to escape left and was very relieved to do so! Take the second gulley. Near the top there is a narrow gap between large boulders that provides some sport. The main gulley is to be the means of descent. There are excellent views from the top, looking back beyond Derwent Reservoir to Back Tor and Dovestone Tor (1).

From the edge of the plateau, head 220° towards a large boulder on the distant horizon. Use the groughs for easier passage. From the boulder, follow a grough which goes SW, to the southern edge of the plateau. You should arrive to the west of Upper Tor. The total distance across the plateau is 1km. There is a gulley 400m west of Upper Tor. Look for an outcrop 60m east of this gulley (2). A small amount of wreckage from a Wellington bomber lies 20m below the plateau edge. Map ref: 110875 (11061/87538). A cross marks the few pieces of metal. A memorial plaque is attached to a rock above the wreckage. It crashed in 1941 with one survivor. The plaque says that the aircraft was returning from a raid on Cologne to its base at Snaith.

Now go east along the edge past Golden Clough (125876). Early one summer's morning I saw an owl flying below the escarpment. It landed not far from me and stayed for a few minutes. Keep on the edge until a fenced off area above Ringing Roger is reached (3).

The next target is the trig. point to the NE at 129878 (4). However, to find the wreckage of another Wellington, locate a gate at the NE corner of the fence. Map ref: 127875 (12740/87521). From the gate go 60m on a bearing of 060° to the site of the wreck. All six crew survived this 1943 crash. Map ref: 128875 (12805/87556). From here, head 030° for 400m to the trig. point.

Wreckage from a Halifax bomber, which also crashed in 1943 returning to Snaith, this time from a raid on Frankfurt, lies 140m from the trig. point, on a bearing of 120°. Map reference: 130877 (13044/87746). There is more wreckage, and a new memorial cross, 120m from here on a bearing of 150°. Map Ref: 131876 (13101/87634). There were two survivors. At this spot in summer, a baby mountain hare ran between our feet and disappeared into a grough.

Return to the trig. point. A thin path leaves on the east side. Take it to Madwoman's Stones 750m away (5). The bearing from the trig. point to the Stones is 070°. On one occasion we met a woman, perfectly sane, who informed us that from here five trig. points may be seen. I managed only two and that was with binoculars!

From the Stones, head north for 250m to the path along the edge of the plateau. Then go west for 2 km, until you pass the gulley you climbed up. Just 100m further on, is the main Blackden Brook gulley (116884) (6). Scramble down this or use the path alongside it.

Scramble at the top of Blackden Brook

Descend back to the road. On one trip I saw a little greenish-yellow common lizard (8cm long) sunning itself by the bridge over the River Ashop.

# Walk 3. Southern Kinder

**Grade:** Moderate

**Distance:** 11km (7 miles)

**Time:** 4-6 hours

**Starting point/parking:** Car park by the road to Upper Booth, off the Mam Tor to Edale road (107847)

## General Description

An interesting gulley is used for the ascent to Noe Stool. Part of the Kinder plateau is crossed to Crowden Head. From here the route goes to two aircraft wrecks in the middle of Kinder Scout, then to Grindslow Knoll. Descent is by a path to Upper Booth. I did this walk with Malc on Christmas Eve. The ground had a light covering of snow and the plateau was frozen, which made the going easier than normal

## Route

Walk up the valley road past Upper Booth towards Jacob's Ladder. As you pass through Lee Farm look for some wood sculptures carved in sawn-off tree trunks. The last time I was there I saw four, including one of Bart Simpson. There is also a very handy shelter. After 1km, the edge of the open access land Is reached (1). There are signs for the National Trust and Jacob's Ladder. Cross the bridge and, leaving the main path, follow the R. Noe upstream. There is a track on its left to start with.

Walk for 300m past a few young trees, which are protected by fencing, to a large holly tree. Where the stream forks, go right (087864). There is a faint path on the right bank, past some small waterfalls. After 200m take the left fork towards Noe Stool. If the water flow isn't too great you can now start to use the stream bed. There are a couple of small waterfalls that are easily climbed. Then a 15ft mossy waterfall is reached. It is best to bypass this on the right bank. I have climbed up the fall to the right of the centre but it is not a sensible idea. This is followed by a pleasant ascent using the rock steps of the bed until a 20ft sloping wall is reached. If this is dry it can be climbed on the right, though it isn't quite as easy as it looks. In this area I recently saw three

Lee Farm wood carvings

birds that looked like ring ouzels. They flew away from me so I couldn't be sure. I have read that these birds are on Kinder but, if they were ring ouzels, it's the first time I've seen one. Continue to the top of the clough. You should now be 200m from Noe Stool (2). The last time I was here I saw a kestrel hovering over the rock.

Head north for 500m, to the slightly raised watershed between Kinder Low and Crowden Head. Look for a cairn with a post. This is the highest point on the plateau at 2088ft (636m) (3). On a clear day, the trig. point at Kinder Low is visible. Turn east and, curving slightly to the north, aim for the cairn at Crowden Head. If you are lucky this may be visible. If it is cloudy, and if you are as incompetent as the author, you may spend some time, wandering in circles, trying to find it.

The high ground between Kinder Low and Crowden Head is the watershed for the east and west of the country. There are three cairns between Kinder Low and Crowden Head. I make the bearings to be: Kinder Low to 1st cairn 050°; 1st cairn to 2nd cairn 087°; 2nd cairn to 3rd cairn 080°; 3rd cairn to Crowden Head 055°. The first cairn, which has a post, is classed as the 'summit'. Map ref: 084875 (08463/87540). The last time I was in this area, heather cuttings had been spread in an

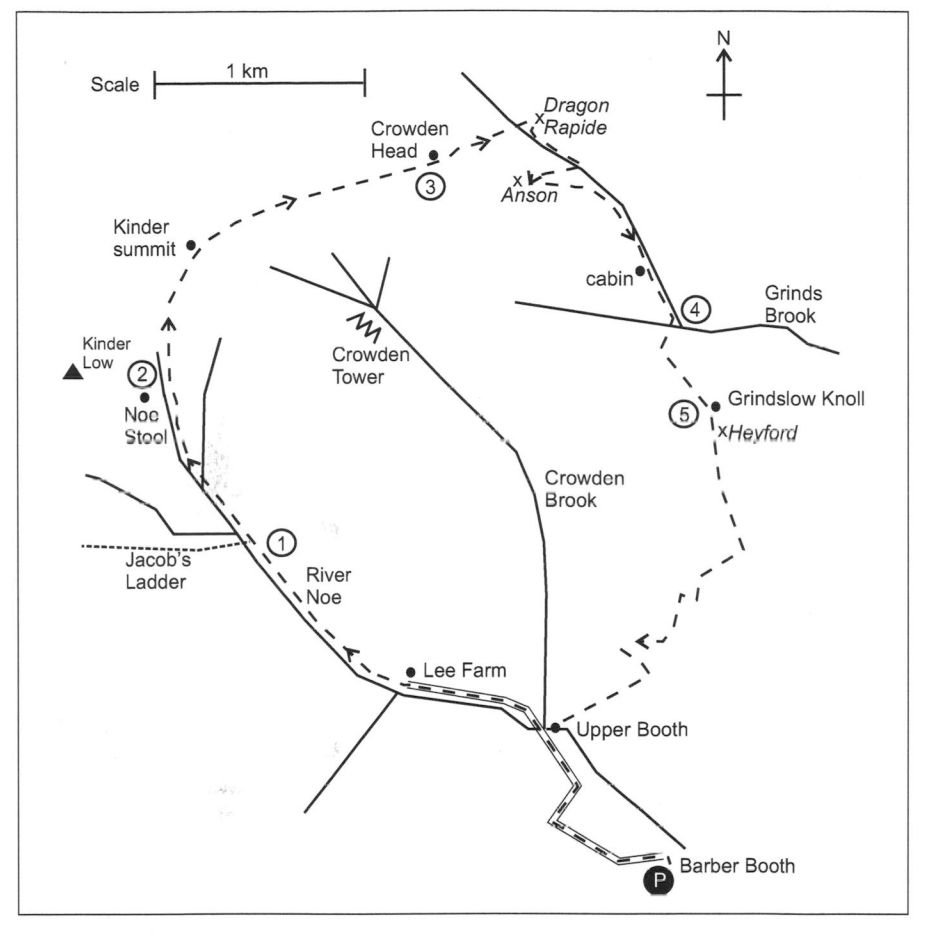

effort to regenerate growth. The map reference of Crowden Head is 095881 (09570/88100).

From Crowden Head the direct route goes on a bearing of 140° to Grindslow Knoll. However, if you wish to have the challenge of finding a couple of aircraft wreck sites, go on a bearing of 075° from Crowden Head. Cross the path that comes up the main gulley from Grindsbrook. Look for some flat rocks less than 100m east of the path. Just below the rocks is part of the engine of a small passenger aircraft, a Dragon Rapide, from 1963. Both the crewmen survived the crash. Map ref: 101882 (10159/88242).

Head SW, back to the path. Go down it for 300m, then west for

200m. Search the groughs in that area for wreckage of a twin-engine trainer, an Anson, from 1944. Map ref: 101878 (10112/87861). It is very difficult to find, although there are two engines and a few other pieces, along with a cross. Again, all the crew survived.

Return to the main gulley and go south past a roofless stone cabin. The ravine at the top of Grinds Brook is not far away (4). Go to the right, along the edge, and follow this round to Grindslow Knoll. From the Knoll go south along a path which drops down, and then crosses flat ground by small pools of water. When you reach a broken wall, 20m to the left and just above the wall, there is a small amount of aircraft wreckage (5). Map Ref: 110860 (11091/86014). This is from a Heyford bomber, a biplane that crashed in 1937. The path goes through the wall and then gets steeper, going SW to the farm at Upper Booth.

On that winter's day, Malc won the mountain hare-spotting competition 2-1. They didn't yet have their full white, winter coats.

# Walk 4. Crowden Head and Brown Knoll

**Grade:** Moderate

**Distance:** 11km (7 miles)

**Time:** 4-6 hours

**Starting point/parking:** Car park (107847), by the road to Upper Booth off the Mam Tor to Edale Road

## General description

The ascent of Crowden Brook offers the opportunity of an easy scramble. As in the previous walk, the line between Crowden Head and Kinder Low is followed, this time in the opposite direction. In cloud this provides an excellent map and compass exercise. The route then goes south along the ridge to Brown Knoll. I first did this walk with Dave in winter with slushy snow on the ground.

## Route

From the car park, take the road to the farm at Upper Booth. Go past a phone box (the last time I passed this way there was a rumour that it may be removed), ignore a path signposted Edale, and cross a bridge. Immediately over the bridge, go through the gate on the right. Now follow the path on the left side of Crowden Brook. There is a farm campsite on the other side of the stream. Open access land is reached 800m from the farm. There is a path by the stream but, where possible, use the bed to ascend.

On the day described, there was snow in the gulley. One can engineer a little bit of easy scrambling on the way, past Crowden Tower, to the plateau. The main path along the edge crosses the gulley here (1). The best bit of scrambling is above this path. Keep going up the rocky bed to where large boulders lie across it. Crawl through the first hole under the boulders. Now, crawl through a second hole, or better still, try to climb over the next obstacle. There is a large foothold on the left at chest height. A third hole is crawled through, followed by a tricky move up and over the next boulder. From here, go north for just under 1km and find the cairn that marks Crowden Head. Map ref: 095881

Crowden Tower

(09570/88100) (2). In the winter this was hard going, through slushy snow-filled groughs. We both plunged into the mire and got thoroughly soaked.

From Crowden Head, aim for Kinder Low on a bearing of 240°, allowing for the curve of the watershed. The three cairns mentioned in Walk 3 should be passed. There is 2km of difficult terrain to cover to Kinder Low (3). Now take the main path south, past Edale Rocks to Brown Knoll (4). This is a further 2km. Near the trig. point Dave went up to his thighs in an icy-cold mixture of mud and slush and needed help to get out. The water poured into a tear near the top of his trousers!

The crash site of an Oxford, a twin-engine trainer, is 200m from the trig. point on a bearing of 300°. This plane crashed on an exercise flight in 1945. Map ref: 081852 (08189/85202). A few years ago the concrete pillar was pushed over. I'm glad to see that it has been restored to an upright position.

From the trig. point follow the path SE for 1.5km passing Horsehill Tor, which lies on the left. On a rather hot morning several years ago Tony L. and myself were walking along this ridge, when three young women coming in the opposite direction, passed us having removed their

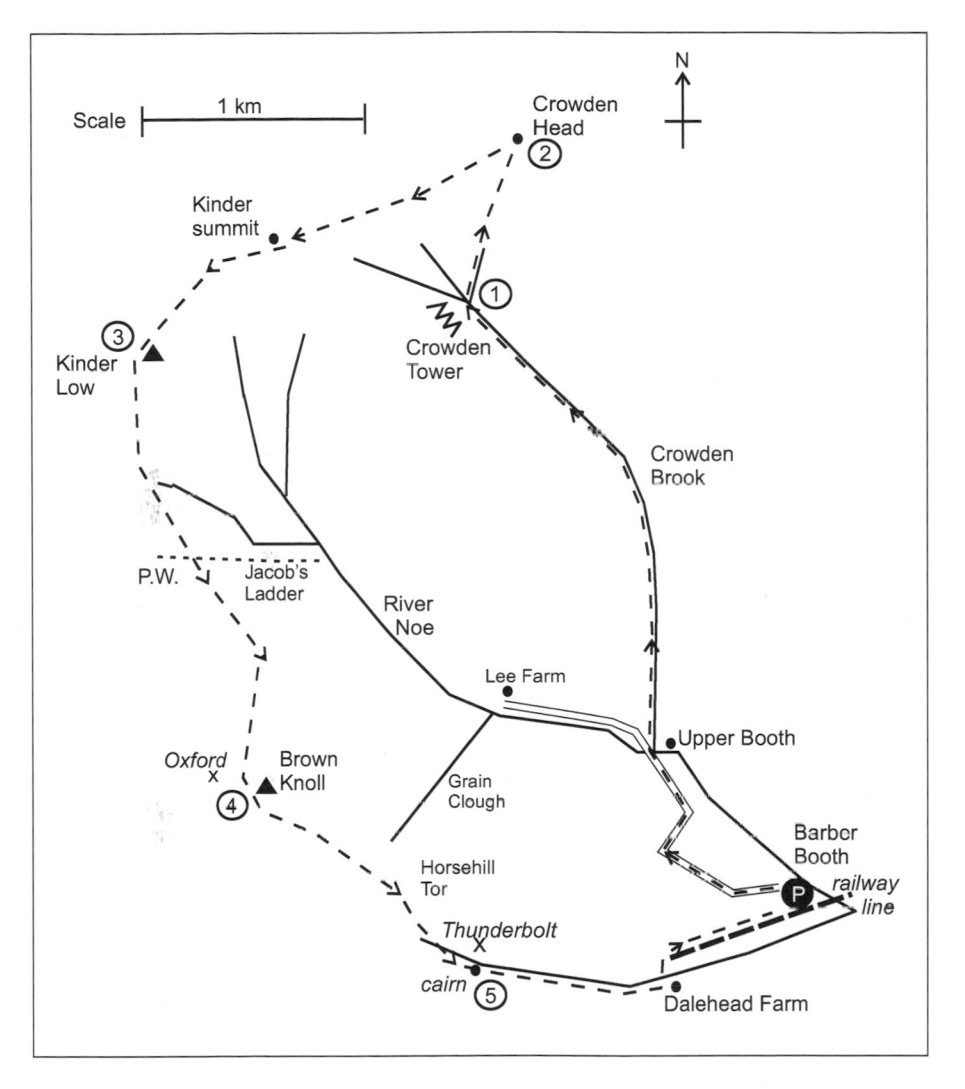

sweaters and shirts. They didn't bat an eyelid! At the top of the gulley, south of Horsehill Tor, there is a cairn and a plaque (5). Map ref: 092843 (09265/84304). This is a memorial to John Charles Gilligan, formerly of the National Trust. It has the words "I will lift up mine eyes unto the hills from whence cometh my help. Psalm 121". Also, less than 100m away, is wreckage from another aircraft. This is from an American Thunderbolt, a fighter aircraft, which crashed in 1943. It is on a bearing of 070°. The small amount of molten metal is at the same height as the cairn. Map ref: 093843 (09356/84338).

Descend from the cairn by the right side of the gulley. The bed is too grassy for scrambling but it is possible to keep close to the clough. When some trees and a rocky outcrop are reached, look out for a mossy water slide. Descend carefully to the right of this. The views down the Edale valley are delightful and the bottom of the mossy slab is a fine place to sit and finish off any food and drink. Keep going down, steeply, to a wall that marks the end of the open access land. Go through the gate in the wall. In July 2005 we spoke to three friendly NT workers/volunteers who were working on the wall. They reckoned to repair 25m of wall in a week. This spot is directly over the Cowburn railway tunnel. The path leads to Dalehead Farm and a NT shelter that contains information boards. Indeed, the belted Galloway cattle mentioned on one board, were encountered in a field by the side of the stony track that passes alongside the north of the embankment. This track leads to the car park at Barber Booth. Back at the car (on that winters day) when we changed out of our sodden clothing Dave, with a gesture of disgust, flung his trousers over the fence.

# Walk 5. Kinder and Red Brook

**Grade:** Strenuous

**Distance:** 17km (10.5 miles)

**Time:** 5-7 hours

**Starting point/parking:** Near Hayfield at Bowden Bridge car park (048869), or free on the road

## General description

Although not long, this walk is challenging. It includes scrambling up and down boulder-strewn gulleys and crossing the deep groughs of the Kinder plateau.

Snake Path sign near Hayfield

It starts with the familiar walk from Bowden Bridge to the Kinder Reservoir; then goes by the River Kinder to Red Brook. This is an excellent scramble up to the plateau. Groughs are crossed to Crowden Head and onto Ashop Edge. Nether Red Brook provides a rocky way down. Rough ground is crossed to the Pennine Way, which leads to William Clough. The Snake Path above Hayfield is a pleasant way to finish the day. I first did this walk in the opposite direction with Dave on a cloudy winter's day in deep, fresh snow.

## Route

The car park at Bowden Bridge is the quarry from which the famous Kinder Scout trespass started from on 24 April 1932. There is a plaque, attached to the rocks at the back of the car park, commemorating this event. Walk along the road towards Kinder Reservoir. It is worthwhile taking the path on the right side of the river, rather than the water board road. On two occasions I have seen dippers flying above the water. Continue to the bottom of William Clough (059887) (1). Take the path that goes to the right between two walls. It leads to a stile 100m away, on the north side of the reservoir. Follow the path eastwards to the end of the reservoir. Then follow the River Kinder, below a wood, using the bank that gives the easiest passage.

At 077884 Red Brook flows down, from the right, into the River Kinder (2). Red Brook is my favourite Kinder scramble. It is a superb route either up or down. In winter conditions it can be quite a challenge. The difficulty depends on the way chosen. Crampons can help when it is icy.

From the top of Red Brook, head east. This means crossing many groughs. If they are filled with soft snow, 'swimming' across them is particularly exhausting as it is impossible to tell how deep they are. The cloud/mist can make it very difficult to distinguish features. After 1.5km you should be close to Crowden Head (3). When visibility is poor, finding the cairn is a real navigational test. Dave and I never found it that winter's day, although we must have crawled all round it.

When you have found the cairn (or not) take a bearing of 290°. If you are lucky, after 500m, you should be able to find one of the groughs that feeds into the main River Kinder grough. This develops into a wide, sandy path and goes to Kinder Gates (088887) (4). These large rocks, on each side of the grough, make a good landmark. Continue in the grough for another 200m, then leave it, heading due north. In 1km Ashop Edge should be reached, hopefully in the vicinity of Nether Red Brook (5).

Use this stony gulley to descend from the escarpment. In summer it is usually dry and straightforward, when there is snow it can provide an entertaining way down. From the bottom, head west, keeping just below Ashop Edge. Wreckage from two jet fighters lies at 072902 (07280/90226). There are some quite large parts, which make it easy to spot from a distance. There is a memorial plaque to the aircrew, Green and Home, who flew the two Sabres. They crashed in 1954. Recently it has been tampered with and parts have been removed. There are more remains on the NW corner of the Kinder plateau. Map ref: 069896 (06921/89643). (See Walk 6.)

Keep going west until the Pennine Way is reached. At 064901, the path down William Clough turns off to the left (6). Descend this until close to

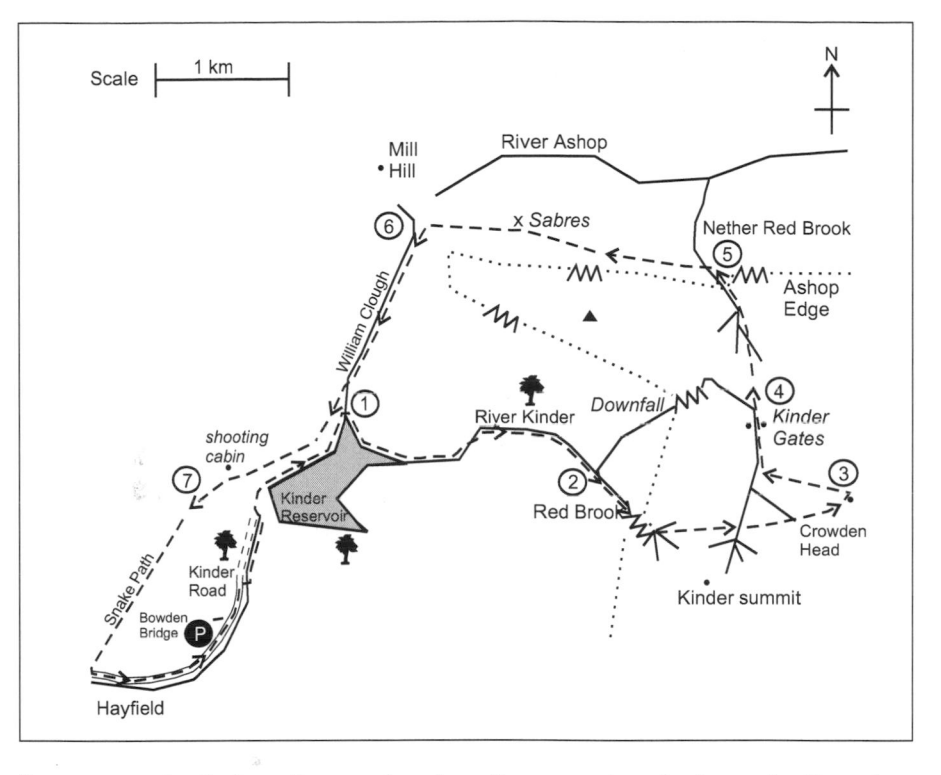

the reservoir. Rather than retracing the way back down to Bowden Bridge, take the path which forks to the right (059889). This path, above the reservoir, climbs slightly to near a white shooting cabin (7). Just below the cabin the Snake Path branches off left. There are excellent views, behind, of the west face of Kinder Scout.

Follow the path for 500m to the corner of a wall and head south, through three kissing gates to Hayfield. Ahead are fine views of Hayfield, Lantern Pike and the Sett valley. The last time I used this path, I saw a kestrel and a wheatear. When the road is reached read the metal sign. Turn left back to Bowden Bridge, passing The Sportsman on the way!

# Walk 6. Northern Kinder and Mill Hill

**Grade:** Strenuous

**Distance:** 19km (12 miles)

**Time:** 6-8 hours

**Starting point/parking:** A624 Glossop to Hayfield road, 1 km north of Little Hayfield. On a bend by Lanehead Road there is a space for 4 or 5 cars (032890). This is 500m south of a gate opposite Carr Meadow Farm.

## General description

This walk is mainly off paths, using beds of small streams for ascents and descents. The route goes over Mill Hill and Featherbed Moss. It then crosses the River Ashop and rises to Fairbrook Naze at the east end of Ashop Edge. The plateau is crossed to Kinder Downfall. Mill Hill is revisited and a different stream, than that at the start, is used for the way down. This walk is hard work over ground that is usually wet.

## Route

From the car park, walk north along the road for 500m. Go through the gate opposite Carr Meadow Farm (035895). Close to the gate, the footpath crosses Hollingworth Clough. By the bridge there is a plaque to the memory of Thomas Boulger of the Peak & North Counties Footpath Preservation Society. Instead of taking the footpath, follow the water upstream (1). There is a sheep track on the right bank. The open access land goes round the wall of Tom Heys Farm. The first 500m is difficult, passing through bracken, but it is worth persevering. This delightful little stream provides a direct route to Mill Hill. It does require some nimble footwork in crossing from one bank to the other. The stream bed may be used, though the mossy, sloping slabs can be slippery.

After 1km, a 15ft waterfall is bypassed. At (056902), a distance of 500m from the top of Mill Hill, leave the clough on the left side and climb up to the path to Mill Hill from Burnt Hill. Just before you reach the top of Mill Hill, at 057905 (05733/90597), there is considerable wreckage of an American Liberator, a four-engine bomber, that crashed in

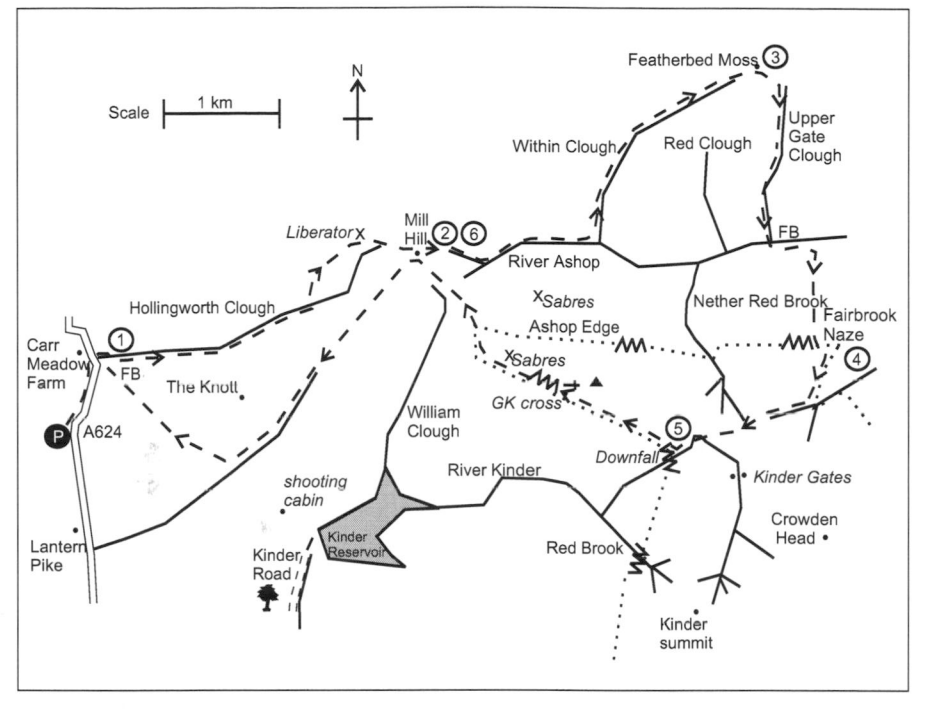

1944. It is spread over a wide area. Somehow the two crewmen survived. Continue to the top of Mill Hill at 1785ft (544m) (2).

Go east for 400m, dropping down to the path along side the River Ashop. Follow the river eastwards for 1km, to the start of Within Clough (077906). Head north up this clough, using the stream bed where possible. Follow this for 2km. The clough ends 200m from the summit of Featherbed Moss (3).

From the top, head 160° for 400m to Upper Gate Clough. Descend this down to the River Ashop. There is a path by the grouse butts. Cross the river and go east along its side for 400m (095907). Then go south, ascending another clough that has a line of grouse butts its side. Continue upwards, aiming for the tip of Fairbrook Naze (4). Scramble up the rocks onto Ashop Edge and go round Fairbrook Naze. Keep on the edge for 800m until you are at the top of Fair Brook. Choose a grough that heads west. The idea is to cross the plateau to Kinder Downfall, 1km away. The River Kinder is likely to be met before the Downfall (5).

Go to the right of the Downfall, along the path on the edge of the escarpment, towards Mill Hill.

At Sandy Heys there is a cross, painted on a rock. This is 800m from the Downfall, near the top of a path that makes a good short cut to Kinder Reservoir. Map Ref: 072892 (07284/89210). The rock overlooks a climb and is on an outcrop that gives a good view of the reservoir. The letters G K are painted by the cross. These are the initials of George King, an Englishman, who founded the Aetherius Society. The society believes that certain points on special hills and mountains are charged with spiritual energy. The "X" marks this spot on Kinder. According to their internet web-site, there are 19 such hills or mountains in the World. One report claims that Coniston Old Man is also one of these sites.

Some wreckage of a Sabre lies 50m to the right of the path at the NW corner of the plateau – map ref: 069896 (06921/89643). This is from the two aircraft mentioned in Walk 5. Take the Pennine Way off Kinder and across to Mill Hill (6).

From here take a bearing of 220° for 1km, through heather, over Leygatehead Moor. Once, in winter we saw a short-eared owl on the moor. Find the start of a clough that leads SW down the moor. Lower down, a track by grouse butts provides the easiest

Sabre engine below Ashop Edge

route. The top one has the number 10. At 046887 a path crosses the clough and leads back to Carr Meadow Farm.

# Section 2: Bleaklow

There are two points in this area that are recognized as 2000ft peaks. These are Bleaklow Head 2077ft (633m) and Higher Shelf Stones 2037ft (621m). The other main features are the Wain Stones, Bleaklow Stones, Hern Stones, Grinah Stones, Barrow Stones, Alport Castles and the infant River Derwent. The main paths are: the Pennine Way, which goes from the top of the Snake Pass in the south to Torside and then towards Crowden in the north; Doctor's Gate, which goes east from Glossop, and the long path from Bleaklow Stones round Howden Edge to Margery Hill.

The four routes from Longdendale start along cloughs that give the opportunity of scrambling (all of the more difficult parts can be bypassed). Then the walks cross bleak moorland, gaining height gradually.

Two routes start in Glossop. Both these visit Bleaklow Head and some travelling along cloughs is involved. Another route starts from Howden Reservoir, exploring the area to the east and south of Bleaklow Stones. This is mainly on open moors. The last route starts from the east side of the Snake Pass and circumnavigates Alport Dale, again, mainly across moorland.

Note: all the map references in this section lie in an area with the prefix SK.

# Walk 7. Higher Shelf Stones and Ashton Clough

**Grade:** Easy (if Doctor's Gate is used)

**Distance:** 14km (9.5 miles)

**Time:** 4-6 hours

**Starting point/parking:** Turn off A57 at sign 'OLD GLOSSOP' by the Commercial Inn. This is Manor Park Road. Turn right in front of The Queens and drive down Shepley Road. Go past the factories and park on the side of the road nearest the river, close to the turning circle for buses (046948).

## General description

This walk uses Ashton Clough for the ascent to James Thorn. It then goes to Higher Shelf Stones on Bleaklow. It returns by the Pennine Way and Doctor's Gate. The route is mainly on paths or easy ground. There is wreckage from three aircraft to be found. An alternative, longer return route is given.

I can recall doing this walk at Easter with friends, Mike, Tony and Willie, when there was still snow on the ground.

## Route

Go east from the parking place along a wide track, with Shelf Brook on the right. Continue on this path, Doctor's Gate, for 3km. A footbridge, with an inscription to Edwin Ambler of The Ramblers Association, is crossed. After a further 40m the path bears away from Shelf Brook (075940) (1). Leave the path and follow this attractive brook, walking along its banks, for 500m to the beginning of Ashton Clough (080941). There are two trees marking the start of the clough. A C47 transport plane crashed on James Thorn in June 1945 and wreckage from it, and a jeep it was carrying, is scattered along Ashton Clough. The first pieces of metal are found near the start and an engine lies a few metres further on.

After 100m a 15ft, mossy waterfall can either be climbed or by-passed. More steps, in the bed of the gulley, are easily climbed.

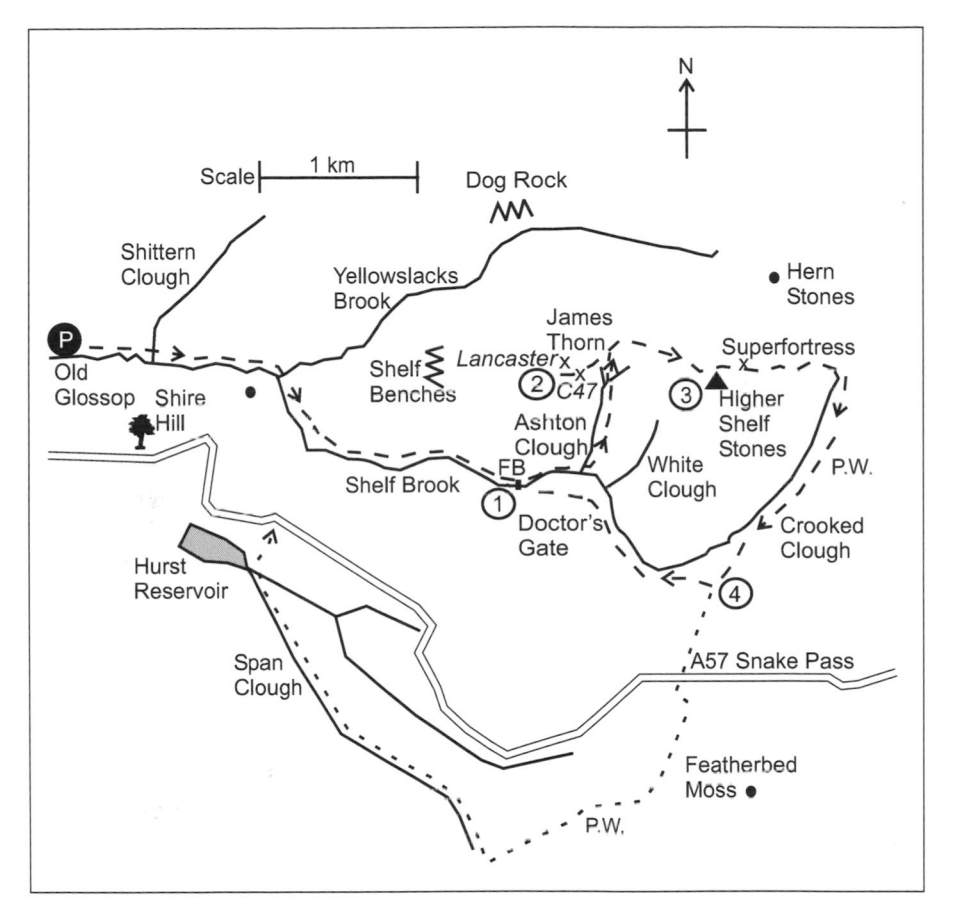

Wreckage, including a wheel from the jeep, is passed. Where the clough forks, take the left branch. Above here, 30m on the left, is part of the undercarriage of the aircraft (08139/94634). Continue up the gulley. At the top turn left and contour round to James Thorn (2). Near the end of the spur are more remains of the C47. Map ref: 080947 (08051/94733). Close by, at 079947 (07921/94784), is a memorial plaque and some remains of a Lancaster bomber. It crashed just a little earlier than the C47 in May 1945. The plaque lists the crews of the two aircraft. A new plate was added in 1995 to commemorate the 50th anniversary of the crash.

Retrace your steps east, and follow the edge past Lower Shelf Stones to the trig. point at Higher Shelf Stones (089948) (3). Near the

The memorial on James Thorn

trig. point, 150m to the NE at 090948 (09066/94878), is the crash site of an American bomber, a Superfortress. There is a memorial plaque to the 13 crew, and a lot of wreckage, including the engines. From here go east and take a path that leads downhill, across the top of Crooked Clough, to the Pennine Way. Follow the Pennine Way for just less than 2km. Doctor's Gate crosses the P.W. before the Snake Pass is reached (4). It is named after Dr J. Talbot of Glossop. It was the old Roman Road linking Melandra at Glossop with Navio at Hope. Doctor's Gate provides a popular and easy way back to Old Glossop.

If you're feeling energetic, here is the description of a longer (by 3km), alternative return route. Cross Doctor's Gate and continue on the P. W. Cross the Snake Pass. Keep on the P.W. for a further 2km towards Mill Hill, until close to the top of Span Clough (075917). Turn north and use the clough bed to descend down to Hurst Reservoir. I have seen snipe along Span Clough.

Lower down the clough it is a pleasant, gentle descent. The open access area ends at Hurst Reservoir. There is a locked water board gate. One option is to use the open access area to reach the A57, 250m away. To do this, follow the wall up the hill to the right and then round to the left. The other option is to squeeze past the gate and follow the track alongside the north side of the reservoir and by the side of the golf course. This is not a right of way, but there isn't a 'Keep Out' sign on the gate. There is a sign near the dam asking you to keep your dog on a lead. I have used this track several times and met other people on it. The golfers have always been friendly. The track joins a minor road. Turn right to get to the A57 and walk back into Glossop. That day in Easter, we retired to the Prince of Wales in Glossop for refreshment.

# Walk 8. Wildboar Clough and Torside Clough

**Grade:** Moderate

**Distance:** 10km (6 miles)

**Time:** 4-6 hours

**Starting point/parking:** Torside Information Centre (068983) by the B6105 off the Woodhead Pass near Crowden

## General description

The approach is via Wildboar Clough and the route continues over open moor to Bleaklow Head, returning by Torside Clough. Wildboar Clough is an excellent scramble and, in winter conditions, can be quite difficult. In summer Torside Clough is particularly pretty. One aircraft wreck is visited. I first did this walk on a summer's evening with Dave and Tony L.

## Route

Go east along the Longdendale trail for 250m to a signpost for Wildboar Clough (1). Follow a path, through trees and bracken, to the bottom of Wildboar Clough. When you emerge from the trees enter the clough. In normal conditions it is possible to scramble up the stream bed nearly all the way to the top. Three rock walls are met. The first may be climbed on the left, à cheval! The second is best climbed to the right of centre. The third obstacle is a 25ft waterfall. This is climbable, but it is safer to bypass it by a chimney on the left. I have climbed the right side of the waterfall but would not recommend it. The rock is slippery near the top and I feel that a rope is advisable, preferably from the top. The rest of the clough presents no problems, apart from an 8ft step which is climbed on the left. On a recent winter's trip a couple of the easier sections had to be bypassed due to ice.

At the top follow the clough SW for 800m to a fork in the grough. There is a stile ahead at 086972 (08675/97211). In a wide grough, 400m SW of here is the wreckage of a Blenheim, a twin-engine bomber that crashed in 1939. There is also a memorial plaque to its

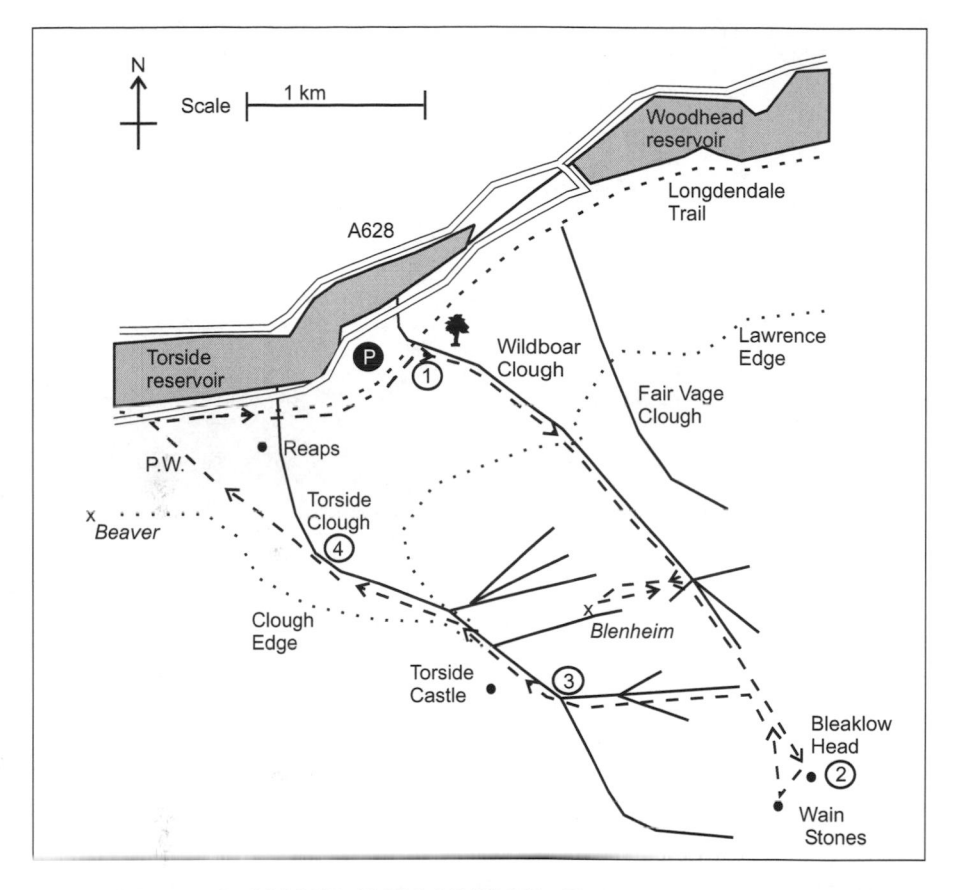

crew. Map ref: 083970 (08304/97008). There is a faint track in the grough that leads to it. This starts above the site at 086968 (08674/96860) and heads on a bearing of 310°. There is further wreckage at 08454/97007, 08205/96901 and 08086/96967. After this diversion, go back up the grough in which the wreckage lies. Then go SE for 400m to meet the P.W. (Pennine Way). At this point it is running east-west. Either follow this east then south to Bleaklow Head, or head directly to the cairn on 160° (2). Just 200m away, on a bearing of 230° from the cairn, are the Wain Stones.

For the return journey, first follow the P.W. back north and then west for just over 1km until you reach Torside Clough (3). The last time I walked along the path I saw a pair of wheatears. The P.W. goes above the clough, however it is dull and Torside Clough is lovely. The stream

Torside Clough

bed presents no real difficulties and has cascades, channels, small waterfalls, narrow gorges and water flowing over flat slabs. People trudging along the P.W. have no idea what they're missing. Even in August a reasonable flow of water may be expected. Look out for dippers lower down the stream.

On that first visit my friends and I all ended up soaked after slipping into various pools of water. If you end up with dry feet you haven't really tried!

Eventually a concrete channel that extracts water is reached and the best part of the clough has ended. A good track is found on the left bank. This joins the P.W. and passes above the buildings at Reaps (4). I believe this used to be a maggot farm – there certainly used to be an interesting aroma around here. The P.W. takes you away from the Torside Centre car park before joining the Longdendale Trail. I have followed the rocky bed all the way down to the Trail. It involves hard work through bracken and climbing over a fence. The longer way is better.

Note: 1km from the P.W. above Reaps there is a small amount of wreckage from an American light aircraft, a Beaver, which crashed in 1956. The wreckage lies just below the top of Bramah Edge and is marked by a stake. Map ref: 055976 (05533/97592). It is just west of the line of the Torside Reservoir Dam wall.

# Walk 9. Bleaklow Head and Shining Clough

**Grade:** Moderate

**Distance:** 10km (6 miles)

**Time:** 4-6 hours

**Starting point/parking:** Take the B6105 off A628 Woodhead Pass and park at the southern end of Woodhead Reservoir Dam (082994).

## General description

Shining Clough is ascended to Lawrence Edge. Shining Clough Moss is crossed to Bleaklow Head and is re-crossed to Lawrence Edge. The descent is by Fair Vage Clough. Shining Clough is a very entertaining scramble. The moor above is bleak and pathless. A diversion is made to look at a classic rock climbing area. Also an aircraft wreck may be visited.

## Route

From the end of the dam walk 300m down the road towards Glossop and turn left under a railway bridge. Follow this track for 1.5km, towards The Lodge, until you reach a sign, "To Open Countryside". Take this path by a wall, to a small ornamental pond. A fence has to be climbed, but there is a sign saying that this is to keep sheep out – not people! Now drop into nearby Shining Clough. There is easy scrambling on rock that is a mixture of crumbling shale and good boulders. After 300m an imposing, overhanging waterfall is confronted. This is best given a wide berth on the left-hand side, on the steep heathery bank; the wider the berth, the safer. However, try to regain the clough as close to the top of the waterfall as possible. The scrambling above the fall is on excellent rock. Soon there is a short vertical wall, but there are good holds on the left. Continue up the clough. There is one final, small four-foot ledge that provides a nice mantelshelf move.

You could continue south across the moor to Bleaklow Head but a visit to Dowstone Rocks is worthwhile. Having finished the ascent of Shining Clough look for the path that travels along the top of the escarpment (1). This path goes along Lawrence Edge. This edge is a fine walk with lovely views. Follow it east for 300m past the top of an outcrop. Take a short, easy angled gulley, on the east side of a high, vertical face. This face is East Buttress. The climb up the crack near the edge of the buttress is called "Phoenix", first climbed in 1947. This is a classic 'Very Severe'. The crack leads to a circular hole in the blank face. This climb is mentioned in Jim Perrin's biography of the rock climber Don Whillans, The

View from the top of Shining Clough

Villain. If you go further round to the west you will find a freestanding pillar, called The Pinnacle. The easiest route up this is classed as a moderate climb. Getting up is OK, but I find the first move coming down unnerving.

Go east, keeping below the outcrop, until you see an old quarry road. Take this for a few metres and you will see Stable Clough. This is usually dry and gives an easy ascent back up to the escarpment (2).

(Optional diversion: At a spot 600m to the east of Stable Clough is the crash site of a Wellington bomber from 1943. There is a little wreck-

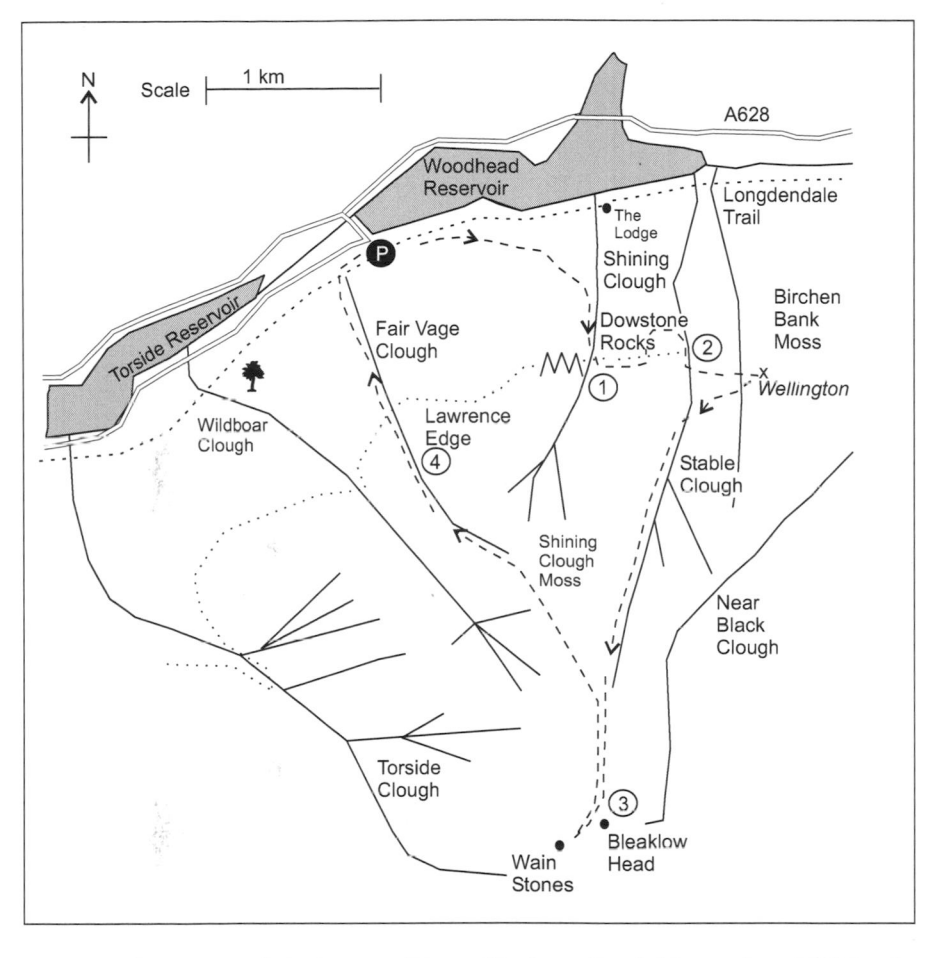

age and a memorial plaque. It is on Birchen Bank Moss about 800m to the west of Near Black Clough. The map ref. is 105985 (10544/98578).

Stable Clough continues southwards and provides a good route across Shining Clough Moss. Aim south towards Bleaklow Head, using the easiest looking groughs. It is 3km from the escarpment to Bleaklow Head – in a straight line!

The large cairn at Bleaklow Head has a post (3). The Wain Stones are 200m away. On a misty day I heard a strange tapping noise between the Stones and Bleaklow Head. On investigation, I found a ranger chiseling a Pennine Way arrow on a stone marker.

The return route gives an opportunity for compass practice. The target, back on Lawrence Edge, is Fair Vage Clough.

From Bleaklow Head, aim north. First cross groughs that feed into Torside Clough and then ones that lead into Wildboar Clough. If you're lucky, by going NW over Shining Clough Moss, you'll find a grough that leads to the top of Fair Vage Clough (4). If you fail it is easy to walk along the Lawrence Edge until you find it (assuming you know which way to turn). It always seems a long way to the edge and there is a feeling of relief if you end up anywhere close to your target.

Fair Vage Clough is usually dry. The rock is a bit loose and care is needed on a couple of steep steps. Low down, a fence is reached. Turn right, over rough ground, down to the track where the walk started. The going underfoot is unmentionable. Fortunately it is only for 400m.

# Walk 10. Bleaklow by Near and Middle Black Cloughs

**Grade:** Moderate

**Distance:** 12km (7.5 miles)

**Time:** 4-6 hours

**Starting point/parking:** Car park after a sharp turn off A628, Woodhead Pass, near the Woodhead Tunnels entrance (113999)

## General description

The route goes up Near Black Clough to Bleaklow Head, along to Bleaklow Stones and returns by Middle Black Clough. The lower parts of Near Black Clough and Middle Black Clough are delightful areas. In summer people often picnic by the water. A little easy scrambling is possible if you keep to the stream beds. Navigation from Bleaklow Head to Bleaklow Stones can be tricky in cloud. Deep groughs make for slow progress. Two aircraft wrecks are visited. A diversion to another crash site is possible (also mentioned in the previous walk). Mountain hares are prolific in this area. A good time to see them is in late winter or early spring when they are still white but there isn't any snow. Dippers may be seen flying over the stream below the car park. Lapwings and curlews may also be nearby.

Note: In exceptionally wet conditions Near Black Clough can become impossible to cross until much higher up. Just before Christmas in 2004 there had been considerable rain in the previous 24 hours and it was still raining. The amount of water coming down the stream was a frightening sight. Crossing the stream a friend lost his walking pole. Two months later we returned and found the pole lying above the stream.

## Route

Cross the River Etherow by the bridge below the car park and follow the track round to where Near Black Clough joins the river. If you don't wish to follow the stream there is a path above Near Black Clough. (Look out for a path that goes up the bank just a few metres above the

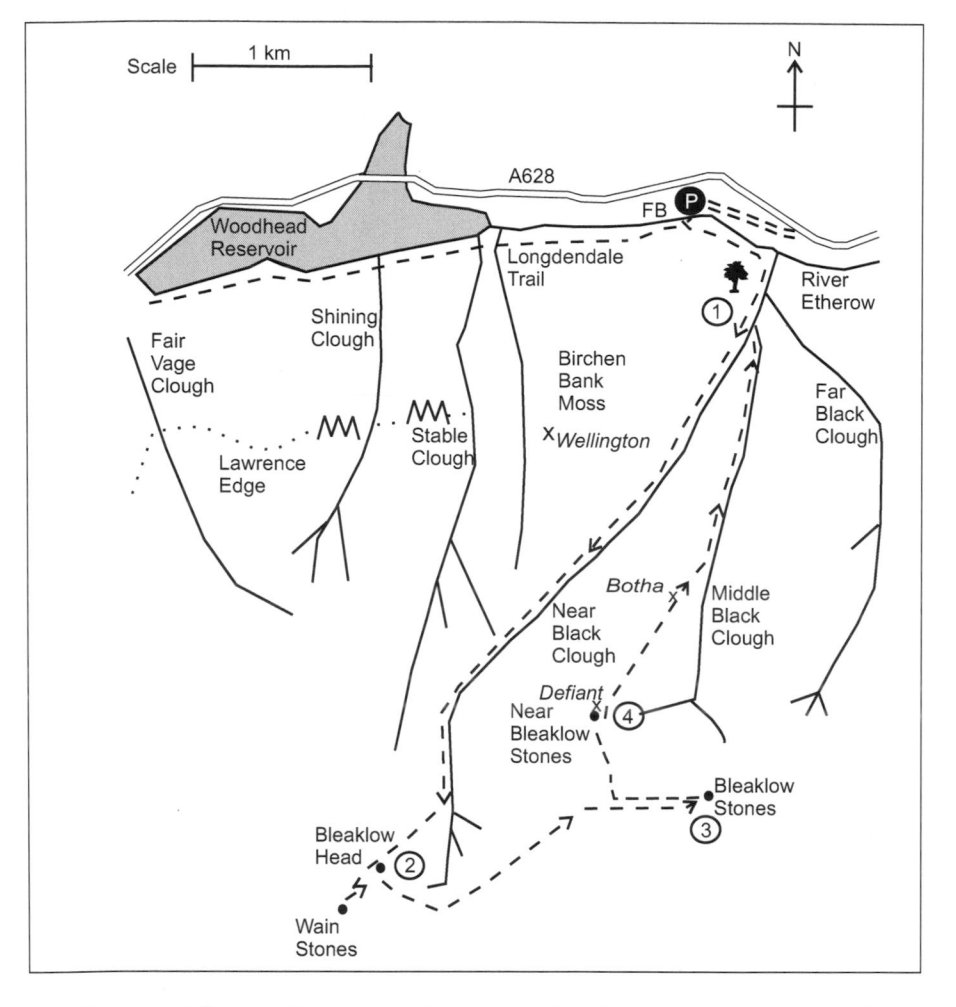

confluence.) The path above the gorge is often very muddy and the attractive surroundings of Near Black Clough are missed.

There is a track on the right bank of Near Black Clough for a short distance, past the confluence with Middle Black Clough (1). Cross to the left side to avoid a steep embankment. Follow the path on this side for 300m. Then, if there isn't too much water flowing, it is possible to use the rocks in the stream bed to make progress. A series of cascades provides a delightful way up. Soon a waterfall with an overhang on the left is reached. Unless it is very dry, bypass this on the right. You can

Near Black Clough

avoid all difficulties by keeping out of the stream but for the more adventurous the rocks provide good entertainment. Further on, a cascade can be climbed on the right. Eventually the angle eases and you find yourself walking along by the side of the stream.

(A diversion to the crash site of a Wellington bomber may be made. It is on Birchen Bank Moss 800m to the west of Near Black Clough. Map ref: 105985 (10544/98578). (See Walk 9))

The main path above Near Black Clough is on the west side. Take this until close to the ridge between Bleaklow Head and Bleaklow Stones. Don't go as far as the high point of the ridge but, just after a fence, look for a path to the right. In mist, good navigation is needed to find the cairn at Bleaklow Head (2). The Wain Stones, 200m away, make a good place for rest and refreshments.

Return to the cairn and then have fun trying to find the optimum route eastwards to Bleaklow Stones. After a while there are stakes that give some reassurance, but it easy to stray off the ridge, particularly to the north. Eventually a reasonable path forms that leads to the Stones (3). There are many weirdly shaped boulders. One is in the form of an anvil while others look like lumbering beasts, especially in the mist. Some entertainment can be had climbing them.

Now retrace your steps west for 500m. Then go north to Near Bleaklow Stones (4). Near here is the wreckage of a Defiant fighter that crashed in 1941. It is just a few metres to the NE of the Stones. Map ref: 106969 (10613/96934). From here go NE towards Middle Black Clough. The considerable wreckage of a Botha, a torpedo bomber, also from 1941, is 700m from the Defiant. Remains of the wings are on the moor 100m west of Middle Black Clough. Map ref: 110975 (11095/97524). Now follow Middle Black Clough north. There is a little scrambling as the descent gets steeper before it joins Near Black Clough. Cross this and return to the car park.

# Walk 11. West of Bleaklow and Yellowslacks

**Grade:** Moderate

**Distance:** 14km (8.5 miles)

**Time:** 4-6 hours

**Starting point/parking:** Turn off the A57 at a sign 'OLD GLOSSOP' by the Commercial Inn. This is Manor Park Road. Turn right in front of The Queens and go down Shepley Road. Go past the factories and park on the side of the road nearest the river close to the turning circle (046948).

## General description

The ascent is by Yellowslacks Brook to Bleaklow Head. The descent is by Shittern Clough. The walk is mainly along stream beds, groughs and reasonable paths. Although the approach is a bit tiresome, it is well worth the effort. The target is to get to the open access land by Yellowslacks Brook. Unfortunately there is no access to the bottom of the brook. There used to be a problem of access to rock climbs by Dog Rock. To discourage climbers the rock face was somewhat modified by dynamite in 1963. However, new routes were put up on the damaged part. With typical climbers' humour, the names include TNT, Master Blaster, Blast Off and Shepherd's Delight (after the name of the person responsible for the damage).

## Route

Go east from the parking place, along the wide track with Shelf Brook on the right. Continue for 2km along the track, passing the path towards Mossylee Farm. At 064944 take the left fork along a wall (1). Don't go up to Shelf Benches, but keep north, staying close to the wall. There is a path for a while but then it peters out and rough ground has to be crossed. This is the worst part of the walk. A fence consisting of a single strand of barbed wire is encountered. Follow this until it crosses to the left bank of Yellowslacks Brook (067951). Now the bed of the brook may be followed all the way to the top.

After 500m there is a new fence across the stream, with a gap in the

Yellowslacks. Climbs made by TNT (see page 43)

top rail. At 078956 is a 25ft slimy wall. Avoid this by using the dry gulley on the right. Near the top of this is a ledge that leads back to the main gulley. In a further 20m there is another 15ft waterfall. This can be climbed either on the right, using knees and a good handhold, or more easily on the left on clean rock. The rest of the clough provides a pleasant route to the top (087954). Here, we were greeted by the call of a golden plover.

Continue along the path by the side of Dowstone Clough as it meanders east, then south. It heads towards Higher Shelf Stones at 088947 (08891/94790) (2). The height of Higher Shelf Stones is 2037ft (621m). This is a popular spot with good views and is a fine place for refreshments. 150m NE of the trig. point there is a large amount of wreckage and a memorial plaque to the 13 crew of a Superfortress that crashed in 1948. The wreckage is spread over a wide area. Map ref: 090948 (09066/94878). Now head 020° for 500m to the Hern Stones (092954). The ground here can be very boggy after rain. There isn't any real path but various sets of footprints will be seen. From the Hern Stones go north for another 500m to Bleaklow Head 094960 (09410/96074) (3). A lot of excellent regeneration work has been done

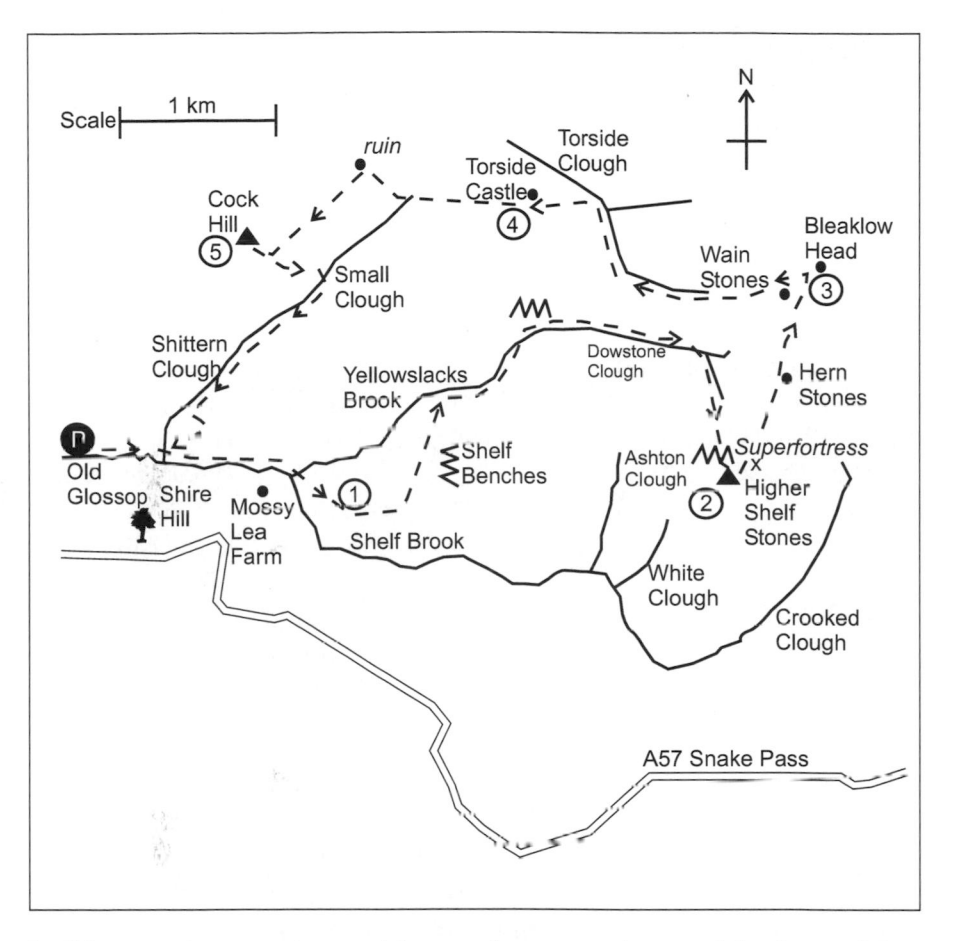

in this area to counter problems of overgrazing, acid rain and fire. Certainly it looks much greener. Grass has been planted to help the more natural heather and cotton grass take root. Find the Wain Stones, at 091959 (09182/95914), which are 200m away on a bearing of 230° from the large cairn and post at Bleaklow Head. Climbing the solitary rock by the Wain Stones can provide a little exercise.

The next target is Torside Castle. Take the clough that goes west from the Wain Stones, rather than the P.W. There is a path along the clough. It starts west then swings north leading, after 1.5km, to where the P.W. leaves Torside Clough. Follow the P.W. north for 80m then take a path to the left (080965). This goes west and after 400m leads to

Torside Castle (4). When we were there in 2005 a new fence had just been erected and a lot of work was in progress on the path. There is a debate about whether Torside Castle was an iron-age fort, a Norman fortification or is simply a natural phenomenon. It is over 80m long and the top is ovoid in shape. The east and west sides of the mound are steep.

Now follow the path west for over 1km. From the stacks of wood we saw, flown in by helicopter, the path should be easy to follow and pleasant to walk along. Cross Small Clough, then the path heads NW up the moor to the ruins of a stone cabin 065967 (06595/96708). Leave the main track and go SW for 800m along a path that passes grouse butts. Look out for a thin path at 060961 (06069/96127) which leads to the trig. point at Cock Hill, 100m away (5). In August 2005 I found two balloons with labels, one from a Stockport school and another, from totally the opposite direction, from a school in York. I often find the remains of balloons in remote places but usually the labels have gone. I suspect sheep find them tasty. There is a path from Cock Hill which leads to Glossop, but a more sporting way is to return east along the thin path and cross the grouse butt track. Keep going east until you can drop into Small Clough. Following this gives a fairly simple rock-hopping way down. The name changes to Shittern Clough. A broken fence is passed, and lower down rhododendrons grow by the stream. When I first came this way 20 years ago they were impassable. Now they aren't a problem. Eventually the open access land ends at a wall. Go left along the wall for 80m to a stile. Climb this and walk down 150m to the main valley track. Turn right, back to the starting point. Grey wagtails may be seen by the stream.

# Walk 12. All The Stones: Barrow Stones, Grinah Stones and Horse Stone

**Grade:** Moderate but in poor conditions it becomes strenuous

**Distance:** 18km (11 miles)

**Time:** 6-8 hours

**Starting point/parking:** Car park after a sharp turn off A628, Woodhead Pass, near the Woodhead Tunnels entrance (113999).

## General description

Far Black Clough is used to climb onto the moor. The route then goes to Barrow Stones, Grinah Stones and over to the bothy by Lower Small Clough. The River Derwent is crossed and the return is by Horse Stone Naze, Round Hill and Lady Cross. The walk is mainly on paths but there are some stretches of pathless moor. After a wet spell the terrain may become boggy. Even in summer you can expect to see mountain (blue) hares on these moors.

Note: After a very wet spell it may not be possible to cross the stream at the bottom of the Black Cloughs. I recommend doing this walk after a dry spell.

## Route

From the car park take the path over the bridge and turn left up the River Etherow. Follow the path, as it turns right, past the ford used by Land Rovers to gain access to the grouse butts. 200m after this, look for Far Black Clough as it joins the main water-course. It is the first branch on the left, and has flat sloping rocks on its right (Map ref:117993). Cross the main stream and follow Far Black Clough. A path starts on the left. There is usually too much water flowing down to use the stream bed here. The path switches to the right side. After 10 minutes or so, a narrow gorge is reached and the steps in the stream bed may be walked up. From here, in normal conditions, the bed may be used for most of the way.

After 1.5km from the start of Far Black Clough the stream becomes too

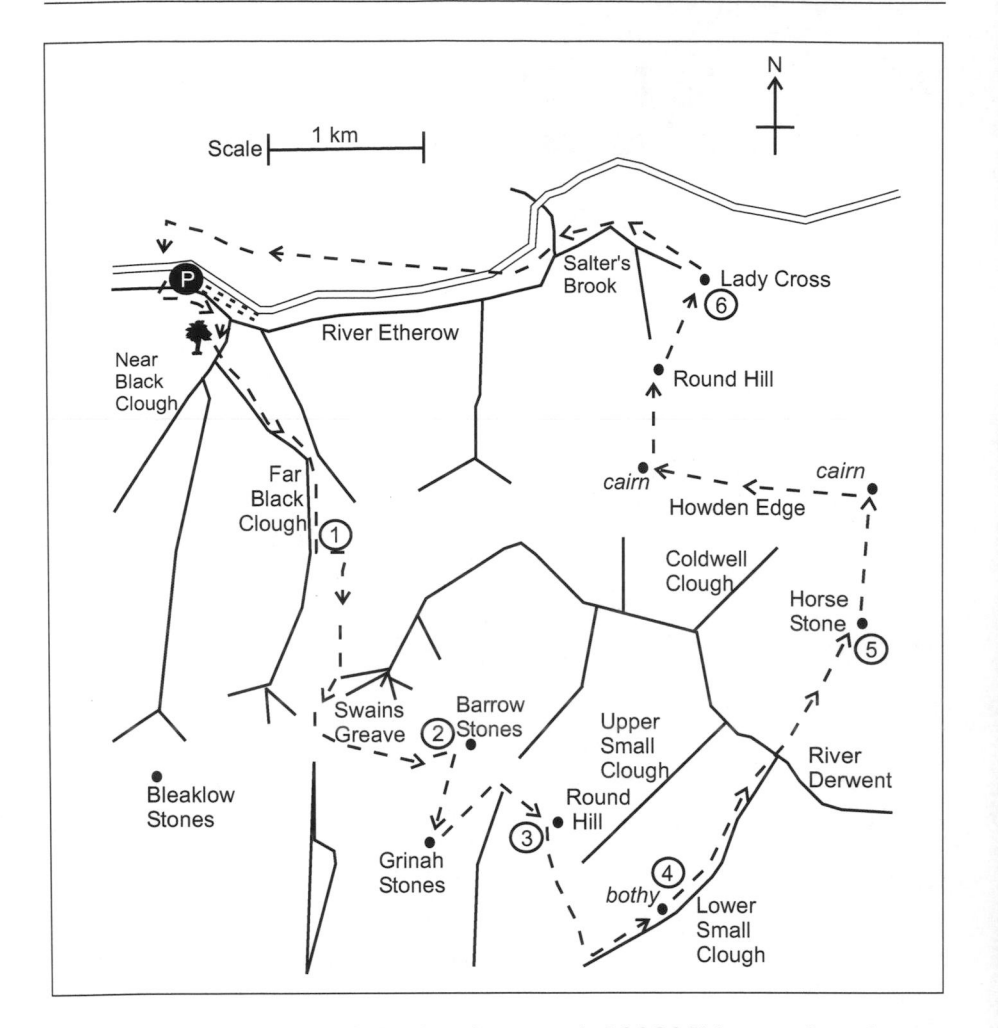

small to be worthwhile following (map ref: 123985) Leave the stream and climb the bank on the left to a good path. This is the continuation of the Land Rover track to the grouse butts. Take the path south for 500m (map ref: 123980) The butts are on the opposite side of the stream. Now go east for 200m, over the heather, or along a sandy grough. The path from Howden Edge is met (1). There are stakes to help you find it. Follow the path up the moor for just over 1km to the top stake (map ref: 124968). The Howden Edge path swings SW towards Bleaklow Stones, but we head east to Barrow Stones. Try to keep to the

Grinah Stones

centre of the ridge. Barrow Stones are 1km from the stake. At the Stones, climbing the group of rocks to the north provides a tricky problem (2). Now go southwards to Grinah Stones. This is a good spot for a rest. The boulder on the edge has a strange hollow in the top. The views from here are excellent. Next return north, back towards Barrow Stones, looking for a new fence on the right. Pass through a gate and take a path leading east, then south to Round Hill 750m away (3). Keep on the path, south, for another 750m. Locate the track that leads down to Lower Small Clough. It is deep and rather ugly, providing access to grouse butts for vehicles. After 500m there are two cabins. The first one is a very neat bothy (4). I visited it on a day after New Year's Eve and got the impression that a group of ramblers had spent the night there. Some festive decorations still adorned the ceiling and a kind soul had left a few chocolate coins. I ate only one, honest! If it is raining this is an obvious place for a rest and something to eat.

From the bothy follow Lower Small Clough down to the River Derwent. The easy option from here is to follow the Derwent to the NW, go up Hoar Clough and past Featherbed Moss towards another

Round Hill. However, if you feel energetic cross the river, then the main path, and climb the slope over rough ground to Horse Stone Naze (5). It's a bit of a struggle, but the views from the top are worth the effort. Go to the Horse Stone, then head north across the moor. The going is relatively easy. After 800m, at 158983, there is a cairn. This is on the Howden Edge path. Follow this path west for 1.5km to another cairn (144987). Take the path north from here for 500m to Round Hill.

Keep on the path to Lady Cross (6). The stone here has the initials I W B carved in it. In good conditions these paths make lovely, easy walking, but when wet ...

From Lady Cross take the path that starts NW then goes west to Salter's Brook. The best route from here is to cross the brook, then the A628 and follow the track west for just over 2km. A signpost directs you down to the Woodhead Tunnels and the car park.

I have tried to follow the River Etherow back to the car park but cannot recommend it, but for the foolish, there is a stile just before the brook is crossed. Sheep tracks may be followed on the left of the river. A fence is reached which has a broken stile. A sign, 200m away, says that it is not intended to keep people out (I mention this to save you the effort of going to read it!) Keep left of the river; the way is rough in places but progress can be made. A 50m stretch of neck-high bracken provides a testing experience. Eventually the Land Rover track up Far Black Clough is reached. I have actually seen a cuckoo here. If there were a reasonable path along the river it would make a perfect finish to the walk, but it is much easier to take the trail to the north of the road.

# Walk 13. Bleaklow Stones from Howden Reservoir

**Grade:** Strenuous

**Distance:** 18km (11 miles)

**Time:** 6-8 hours

**Starting point/parking:** At end of the road (168938) by Howden Reservoir off the A57 Snake Pass. **Note:** Cars are not allowed past Fairholmes on weekends; a minibus service runs instead.

---

### General Description

The route visits Alport Castles, Bleaklow Stones and returns along the infant River Derwent. Much of this walk is on paths though these can be very boggy. Some pathless ground, through heather and bracken, has to be crossed.

### Route

From the parking place, walk back 2.5km along the road by the reservoirs. At the end of the arm of the reservoir, made by the River Westend, cross the bridge. Leave the road and turn right into the Ditch Clough Plantation (155927). After 200m take the path on the left signposted to Alport (1). It goes uphill and after 500m escape from the wood to use a wide track to climb the moor. The track serves nearby grouse butts. After 1.5km, heading SW, the edge above Alport Castles is reached.

Now turn NW along the path above the River Alport valley. The path follows the edge for 1.5km then, at a clough, goes away from the edge. Westend Moor trig. point is reached after a further 500m. Map ref: 128933 (2). Continue NW over boggy ground. In places the path disappears. 1.5km from the trig. point the top of a hill is reached. Follow a bearing of 280°, trying to keep on the high ground. A junction of paths is met at 115946. Go NW on a path that climbs to the start of The Ridge (950112).

At the top of the ridge follow the groughs past some large boulders. The path between Bleaklow Head and Bleaklow Stones is met near a

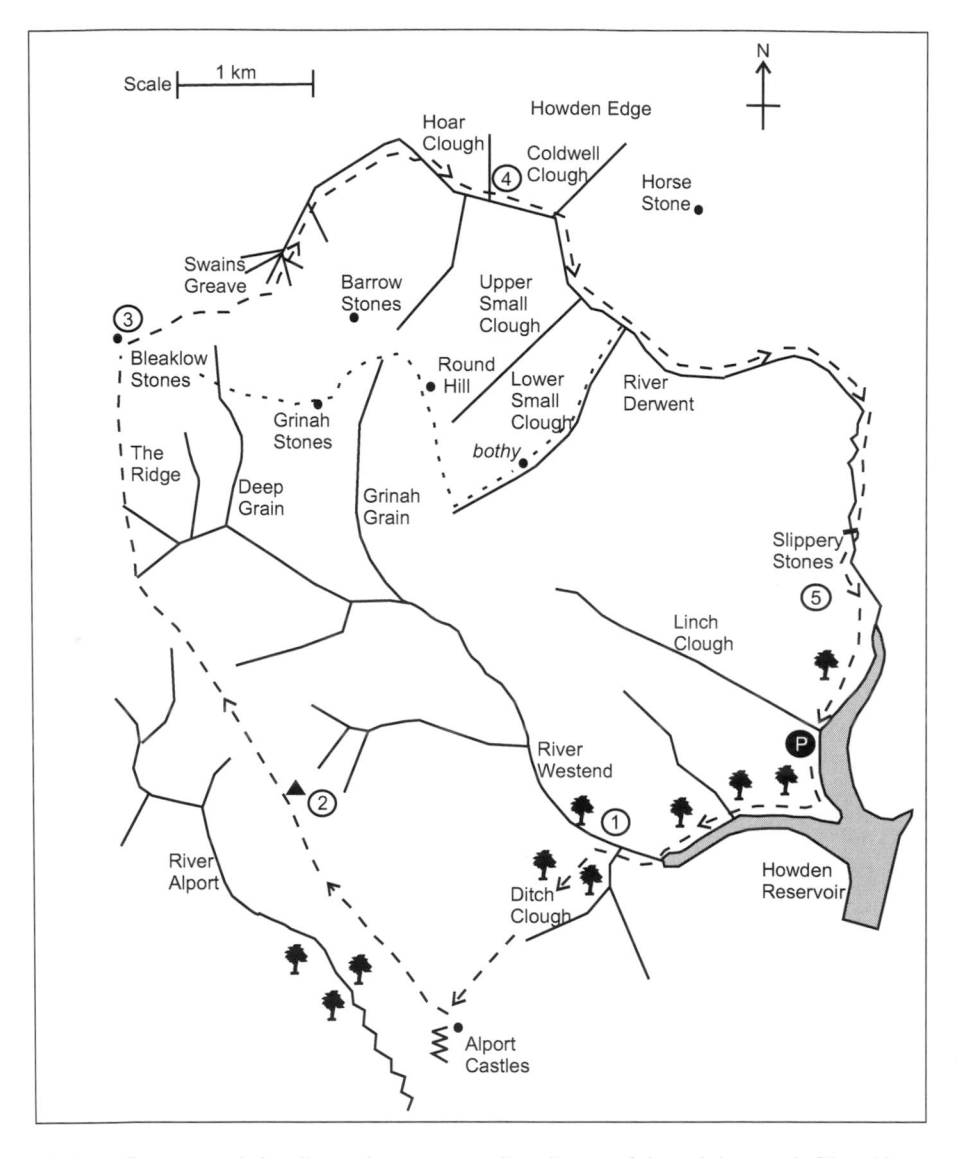

stake. Turn east to the strange collection of boulders at Bleaklow Stones (3). There are lovely views here, particularly from the top of some of the boulders.

From here the aim is to go to the source of the Derwent and follow it to Derwent Reservoir. This means covering some difficult terrain.

Slippery Stones bridge

An alternative is to go east from Bleaklow Stones, looking for a path that goes in the direction of Grinah Stones. This is not the main path that leads through many groughs to Howden Edge. The required path drops slightly, off the high ground, and contours round the southern flank of the moor directly to Grinah Stones. It is a good path, through heather, crossing only a couple of cloughs. From Grinah Stones follow the route described in Walk 12 over Round Hill, down Lower Small Clough, passing the bothy, to a path by the side of the River Derwent.

Those wishing to follow the Derwent from the source, should take a path east from Bleaklow Stones for 300m, then swing left on a bearing of 060°. This leads to Howden Edge. After another 1km, at a stake, leave the path and go NE through the area named on the map as Swains Greave. This is a very boggy area and is the source of the River Derwent. When you leave the path take any small clough, they all feed the infant river. The going by the stream is not easy. There is the occasional sheep track, but bracken and heather have to be forced through.

1.5km from the point where the river is formed, at the bottom of

Swains Greave, a path is reached. This comes down from Hoar Clough, to run above the left bank of the river (143977) (4). After 1km the path becomes a wide Land Rover track. This provides a well-deserved, easy stroll with pretty views of the river. Follow this all the way back to the bridge at Slippery Stones (5). Cross the bridge and return to Howden Reservoir. The distance along this lovely valley is 7km.

On one occasion, as I neared the reservoir a Spitfire flew down the valley, passing low over my head. It was followed by a Chinook helicopter. It was a few days before the Woodford Airshow, which may have explained their presence.

# Walk 14. Alport Moor

**Grade:** Strenuous

**Distance:** 20km (12.5 miles)

**Time:** 6-8 hours

**Starting point/parking:** Small car park, south side of A57, near track to Hagg Farm (163886)

## General description

This walk completes a circuit of the high ground surrounding the Alport valley. It finishes with a nice, easy track above the River Ashop. Some of the walk is on paths but much of it is across boggy land, on either faint or non-existent trails. Alport Castles are visited; these are the result of landslips. The sites of two aircraft crashes are close to the route. One of the best features of this walk, weather permitting, is the view of the surrounding hills.

## Route

From the handy car park, walk a few metres along the road and go up the track towards Hagg Farm. This used to be a Youth Hostel but it is now an environmental centre. Continue upwards until, after a gate, a junction of several paths is reached. This is just before a plantation of trees on the right. In here, there are a few pieces of metal just to the east of a wall at 165890 (16592/89027). This wreckage is that of a Meteor, a jet that crashed in 1950. The pilot parachuted to safety.

At the junction take the path, to the left, which climbs NW up to Rowlee Pasture. After 1.5km the top of Rowlee Pasture is reached. Along this path, there are good views of Lose Hill, Back Tor and Mam Tor to the south. To the east, 450m below the top, and 50m above a broken wall, is a small amount of wreckage from a Defiant fighter aircraft from 1941. A metal strut, stuck in the ground, indicates the position. The two members of the crew also parachuted safely to the ground. Map ref: 154904 (15459/90482) and 152905 (15284/90503). Back on the top continue along to Alport Castles (1). In 2005 peregrine falcons had returned here and nested. The RSPB had a hut there to guard the nest.

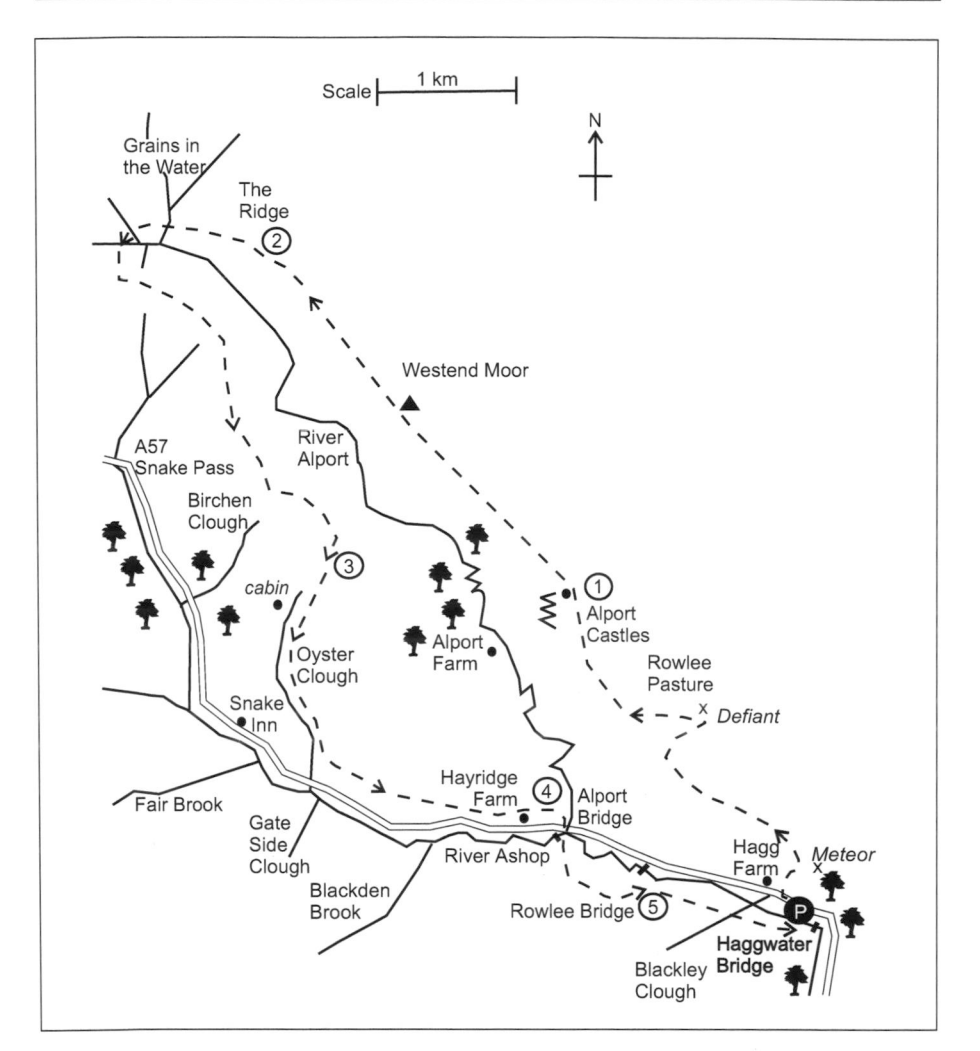

The path continues for another 2.5km to the Westend Moor trig. point.
Along this ridge the panorama is excellent; there is Kinder Scout to the
left, the Bleaklow massif ahead and the Derwent hills to the right. Keep
going NW on a faint path but soon the going becomes boggy and
you have to find you own way across the morass. Keep on the high
ground for a further 3km to the bottom of The Ridge (2). Walking along
here in February I saw several golden plovers. At 112950 turn west and

Alport Tower from below

drop into the bowl where several streams come together and form the River Alport. This area is named 'Grains in the Water'. Map ref: 105948.

Two people died here, suffering from exposure, in 1964. They were taking part in the Four Inns Walk and got lost in appalling conditions.

At this point, one option is to return along the River Alport. It is possible to go down this lovely valley all the way to Alport Farm. The intention is to remove the pine trees and return the valley to its former state, with natural trees. This is expected to take 40 years. Eventually you reach Alport Bridge where the route being described below is joined.

For those willing to face wet, tussocky ground crossed by groughs, climb south out of Grains in the Water onto the ridge on the west side of the River Alport. Continue SW keeping as best as you can to the top of the ridge. Crossing the top of Nether Reddale Clough, I came across a scientific contraption recording data about water flow. The target, which is some 4km from 'Grains in the Water', is Oyster Clough. At 120922, when north of Oyster Clough, turn south towards the clough (3). This is a grouse shooting area.

A good path leads from the shooting cabin (117915) to join the footpath marked on the map as a Roman road, north of the wood above the Snake Inn. Another option is to drop down and descend by the side of Oyster Clough. The stream is quite narrow and there may be a strong flow of water. There are several small but attractive water-falls. Eventually a fence and wall are reached. The hardest work of the walk is now completed.

Take the path left, up the slope by the wall. After 2.5km this path leads to Alport Bridge. There are good views of Gate Side Clough and Blackden Brook, on the other side of the valley. At Hayridge Farm I once saw a large flock of fieldfares. Climb a stile that is 50m above the farm (4) (it is easily missed). When the farm track is reached, go left for 200m, and then take the path on the right, by a post, down to the road. Cross the road and take the signposted path to the bridge/ford over the River Ashop.

Over the river, take the path to Rowlee Bridge 1km away (5). At the bridge there is a signpost pointing east along a culvert. This is a perfect way to finish the walk. The gradient is fractionally downhill, the River Ashop is below and you are away from traffic. The culvert extracts water from the River Ashop and diverts it, via a tunnel, to the Derwent Reservoir. The path leads into a wood and then down to Haggwater Bridge. Cross the bridge and follow the track 250m up to the road and the car park.

# Section 3: Black Hill

Black Hill at 1908ft, 582m, isn't quite 2000 feet above sea level, but it is the highest point in West Yorkshire. Although the summit isn't far from roads to the north and east, it is a long way to civilization in the other directions. The ground is usually boggy. The Holme Moss TV mast is near the A6024 and when visible is a help to navigation. The road between Holme and the Longdendale valley climbs to 524m and is often affected by snow and ice in winter. Other features are Laddow Rocks and the Castles above Crowden Great Brook, Chew Reservoir, the reservoirs near Greenfield and the outcrops above them.

Several brooks cut deeply into the large tract of land to the east of Black Hill. The whole area is surrounded by large reservoirs.

The Pennine Way goes to Black Hill from Crowden in the south, with two alternative routes to the north. There is a path from Laddow Rocks to Dovestone Reservoir, and another going south from Black Hill, over Tooleyshaw Moor to Crowden. Apart from these, there are few paths that cross the moors.

Of the routes described, three go to Black Hill; from Holme, Crowden and Yeoman Hey Reservoir. Routes exploring other parts of the moors start from Dunford Bridge, Crowden, Dovestone Reservoir, and Arnfield.

# Walk 15. Chew Reservoir and Featherbed Moss

**Grade:** Moderate

**Distance:** 13km (8 miles)

**Time:** 4-6 hours

**Starting point/parking:** Dovestone Reservoir car park, off A635 Mossley to Holmfirth. **Note:** there is now a charge for parking during the week (SE013035)

## General Description

This walk starts with a climb up a clough to Wimberry Stones. A path on the edge above Chew Brook is taken to Chew Reservoir. Pathless ground is covered over Featherbed Moss to Ravenstones. The edge above Dovestone Reservoir is followed before a short descent to the car park. The sites of four aircraft wrecks may be located.

## Route

Reaching the open access area below Wimberry Rocks is awkward. From the car park, walk along the south side of the reservoir with Chew Piece Plantation on your right. Take the path, on the right, directly before a bridge over Chew Brook. Walk for 30m, climb up the bank on the right, into the plantation. Continue SW through the wood, past large boulders to a higher path. Go west until a stile at the edge of the wood is reached. The clough that is to be used to climb up to Wimberry Rocks is 50m from the wood.

Although there is a path across this field, it is not open access land. To reach the clough, don't climb the stile, but force your way through bracken for 150m to the SW corner of the wood. Climb over the gap in the corner and go west for 100m over poor ground to the clough (SE015027). Ascend this for 100m, looking out for the wreckage of a Dakota passenger aircraft at SE014026 (01491/02669). The crash happened in 1949. There were 8 survivors but 24 people died. Part of the undercarriage lies in the clough. The gulley provides a relatively easy way to the edge to the west of Wimberry Rocks (1).

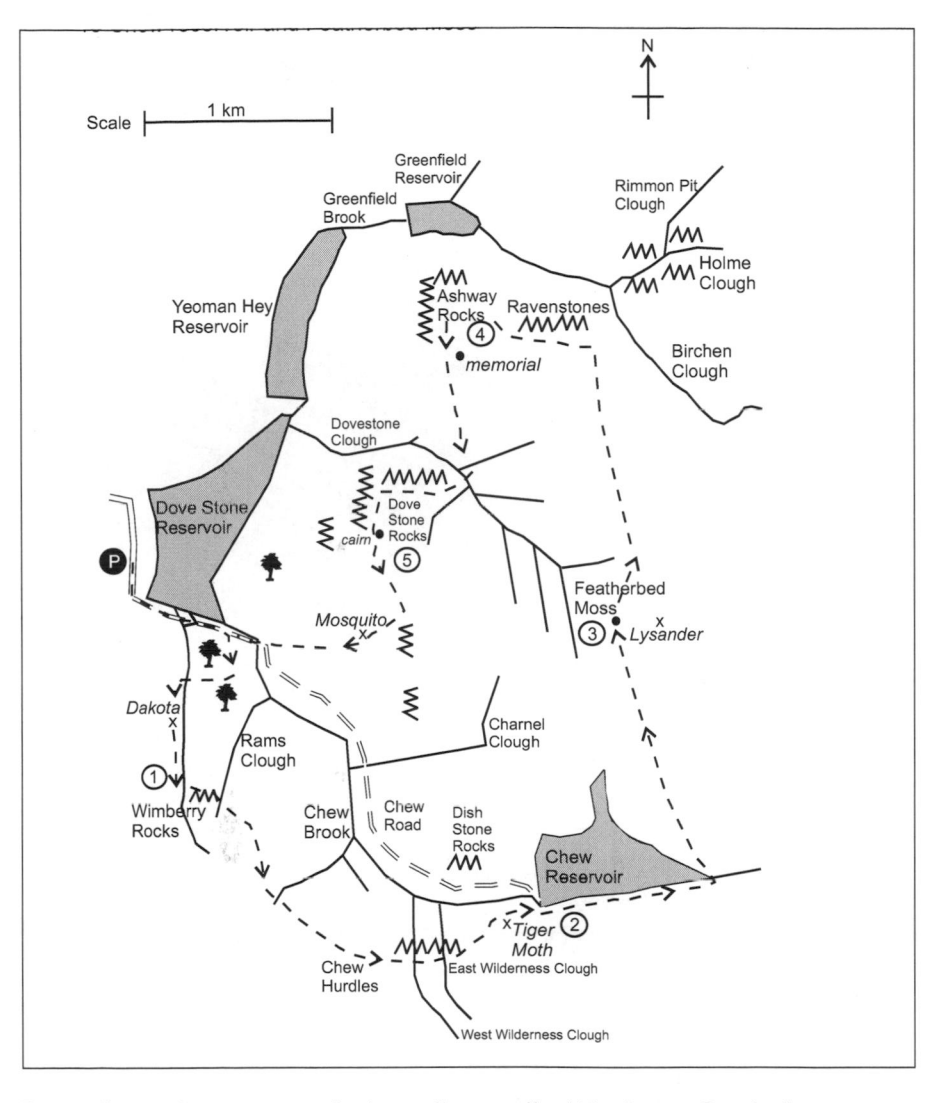

From the edge, go east along the path. Wimberry Rocks has some fine rock climbs. A path leads to bottom of the climbs from the east end of rocks, by Rams Clough. Jim Perrin's book, The Villain, tells of Joe Brown climbing a classic HVS here, called Freddie's Finale. The path to Chew Reservoir curves south and then east, past Chew Hurdles. There are fine views of Chew Brook, Dish Stone Rocks and the moorland to the north. East and West Wilderness gulleys are good scrambles. East is

The Trinnacle, Ravenstones

harder than West. Tragically, two climbers died here in 1963 in an avalanche.

On Blindstones Moss, 300m before Chew Reservoir, is a small amount of wreckage of a Tiger Moth trainer aircraft from 1945. It is above a gulley, 40m before a new fence that runs parallel with, and 100m from the path. Map ref: SE033015 (03353/01585). Walk to the SW corner of Chew Reservoir (2).

Go along the southern edge of the reservoir until its end (SE043018). Walk round the east side of the reservoir and take a bearing of 340° for 1.5km, across boggy terrain, to the summit of Featherbed Moss (SE039032) (3). The height given on the Ordnance Survey map is 522m or 1713ft. From the summit go 200m on a bearing of 080°, to the very small amount of wreckage of a Lysander aircraft that crashed in 1941. Map ref: SE040032 (04069/03245). The two crewmen survived two days on the moor, before being found by a rescue party. Sadly, one of them died from his injuries a few days later. The line to the wreckage from Featherbed Moss is just to the right of the TV mast at Holme Moss (Black Hill).

Now go north across open ground to the edge above Greenfield

Brook. Don't go down Birchen Clough but keep on the edge to Ravenstones (4). The impressive, free-standing pillar with three tops is called the Trinnacle. This is a good viewpoint and a popular spot for photography. The Ravenstones outcrop has some classic rock climbs.

Now, keeping on the edge, go west then south. At SE031044 there is a large cross. This is a memorial to James Platt, an Oldham MP who was killed in a shooting accident in 1857. His brother, John, had a shooting lodge, Ashway Hall, built by the side of Dovestone Reservoir in 1850. It was demolished in 1981. There is an information board by the reservoir, and a set of steps is all that remains. Continue along the edge, cutting in to pass round the top of Dovestone Clough. At Great Dove Stone Rocks there is another memorial (SE025037) (5). It is attached to an obvious rock stack, named Fox Stone. The plaque is to the memory of two climbers, Brian Toase and Tom Morton, who were killed in a fall in the Dolomites in 1972. As you begin to get towards the end of the reservoir, start to angle down the slope. At SE025031 (02569/03184), on a flattish shelf below the steep hillside, is a small amount of wreckage from a Mosquito aircraft that crashed in 1944 returning from a raid on Hamburg. From here, walk directly down to the reservoir.

# Walk 16. Black Hill from Holme

**Grade:** Moderate

**Distance:** 12km (7.5 miles)

**Time:** 4-6 hours

**Starting point/parking:** Holme, in a cobbled 'square' off the A6024 (SE108059)

## General description

The start is along Issue Road, up to Black Hill. The walk continues past the Holme Moss mast and across to Ramsden Clough. The return is past Ramsden reservoir. Many groughs, and boggy ground are crossed. It is possible to visit the sites of three aircraft wrecks.

## Route

From the cobbled area in the centre of Holme, take the track leading NW past a school. This leads to Issue Road. Leave this, after 2.5 km, when the path veers to the north (1). Go up Issue Clough, which lies directly ahead. Rough ground is covered to reach the clough and there is more awkward ground by the side of the clough. Bypass a 30ft waterfall on the right. After a further 50m it is possible to walk up the bed of the stream on crumbly slate. At the top the P.W. comes in from the right. There are paving flags all the way to the trig. point on Black Hill summit (2).

Some wreckage from a biplane, a Swordfish that crashed in 1940, lies 500m east of here. Walk east and take any clough, they all lead to Heyden Head. A fence is met that comes in from the right. Follow this to the junction of several cloughs, from where Heyden Brook falls steeply, SE, off the moor. To find the little that remains of the Swordfish, take the first clough on the left of the one containing the main path (this is with your back towards Holme Moss mast). The wreckage is 60m up the clough. The bearing to the mast from the wreckage is 130°. Map ref: SE083047 (08343/04768).

There is more aircraft wreckage on Great Hill. On a line from Great Hill to Cliff Edge, and about 400m up from the fence at Cliff Edge,

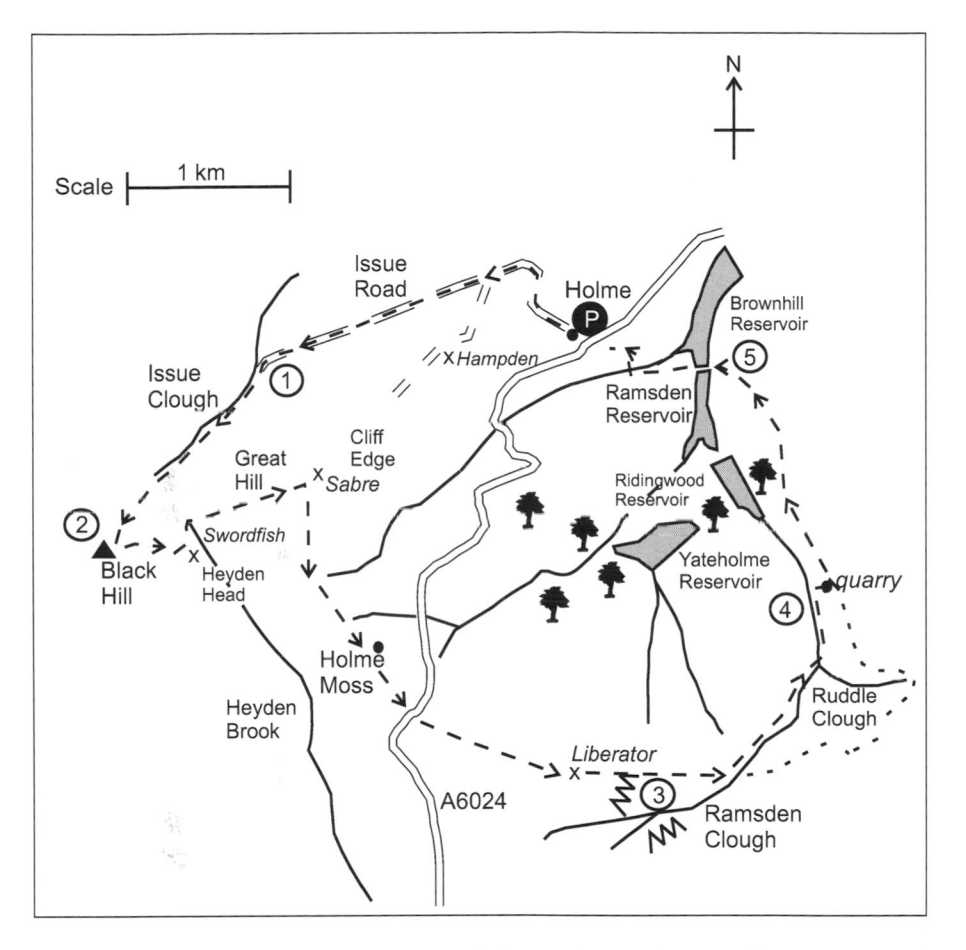

there is a wide area of even ground. There is a cairn marking the site of wreckage from a fighter, a Sabre, which crashed in 1954. Map ref: SE091050 (09100/05070). To get here from the Swordfish site, go round the top of Heyden Brook, heading 080° for 800m. The bearing to the TV mast from the wreckage is 160°. You may pass a concrete post on the way.

Now head for the Holme Moss TV mast, passing it on its right side. Walk SE and cross the A6024 by a lay-by. Step over a fence. Either keep to the top of the ridge going roughly SE for 1.5km, then swing NE to pick up groughs which lead into Ramsden Clough, or keep further north crossing above Lightens Edge to search for the wreckage,

Ramsden Reservoir

mainly undercarriage, of a Liberator which crashed in 1944. Only one member of the crew survived. Map ref: SE106033 (10639/03374). A memorial plaque, dated 2005, has been placed here by the West Dewsbury Scout Group. From the site, go east for 1km to Ramsden Clough (3).

Now there is the choice between a more gentle, longer way down to Ramsden Reservoir or a shorter route over some rough ground. The longer way gives good views, the shorter is perhaps more interesting.

The short way is to go down by Ramsden Clough with its impressively steep sides, past Ruddle Clough, until the end of the open access area is reached at a locked gate (SE122043) (4). There are remains of various old buildings on the way. Unfortunately, the track down to the reservoir is on private land for 1km. But there is a way to an open access point. Climb the right (east) side of the valley for 100m to an old quarry (SE123043). A water board worker told us that this is the site of a old army shooting range.

The easier way to the quarry is to go round the top of Ramsden Clough on a pleasant path which leads to Ruddle Clough, with views back to Black Hill and down to the reservoirs below. From the top of

Ruddle Clough there is another path, just to the north of the clough that drops west for 300m. It then turns north towards the old quarry. The path peters out by a flat rock. Drop down 30m to a sheep track above a fence. This leads to the quarry and meets the way described above.

Walk along the quarry track for 1km to an access point. Go downhill, bearing left when a track is met. At a bend take a path right and immediately left, down to a picnic area by Ramsden Reservoir Dam (5). Cross the dam wall. Brownhill Reservoir is below you. Turn right and follow the path round a small inlet. Then go left up a slope back to Holme.

Note: an alternative, easier way on to Black Hill, from Holme, is to take Cliff Road, which turns left off Issue Road at SE102063, and leads directly to Cliff Edge. Taking a direction directly to the summit trig. point will take you close to the Sabre wreckage. Also, at SE099057 (09919/05751), just over the wall on the left of the path, is the reedy hollow formed by the crash of a Hampden bomber, 1940. There is no wreckage.

# Walk 17. Crowden Great Brook and Crowden Little Brook

**Grade:** Moderate

**Distance:** 13km (8 miles)

**Time:** 4-6 hours

**Starting point/parking:** Crowden car park by A628 Woodhead Pass (SK072993)

## General description

A delightful walk to Black Hill, using Crowden Great Brook for the ascent, and Crowden Little Brook for the descent. You will need to cross the brooks many times to find the easiest passage. I recall doing this alone in January. There was good visibility and a light covering of snow. The temperature was well below freezing and the rocks were icy.

## Route

Take the path past the campsite, keeping Crowden Brook on your left. Go past the weir and the confluence of Crowden Great and Little Brooks. Cross Crowden Little Brook at a footbridge and follow Crowden Great Brook (1). For the first kilometre or so it is fairly open but then the sides get steeper and form a ravine. It is necessary to change banks several times. Some of the rocks are quite dramatic giving the route an adventurous atmosphere. There are good views of Laddow Rocks to the left and the Castles to the right. One winter we saw a mountain hare, in its full white coat, which didn't run away. It stayed perfectly motionless while we stood next to it. If we hadn't seen it from afar it could have been mistaken for a stone but it was too symmetrical and you could just make out the outline of its ears flattened against its back. It was the nearest I'd been to a hare and I didn't have a camera!

After another 2km the Pennine Way comes in from the left. Follow it and its paving flags, to the trig. point at the summit of Black Hill (2). There, I met two people who claimed they could see Pen-y-gent and Ingleborough. They also said they were into white water canoeing. Not much chance of that on Black Hill! The top of the moor had some icy

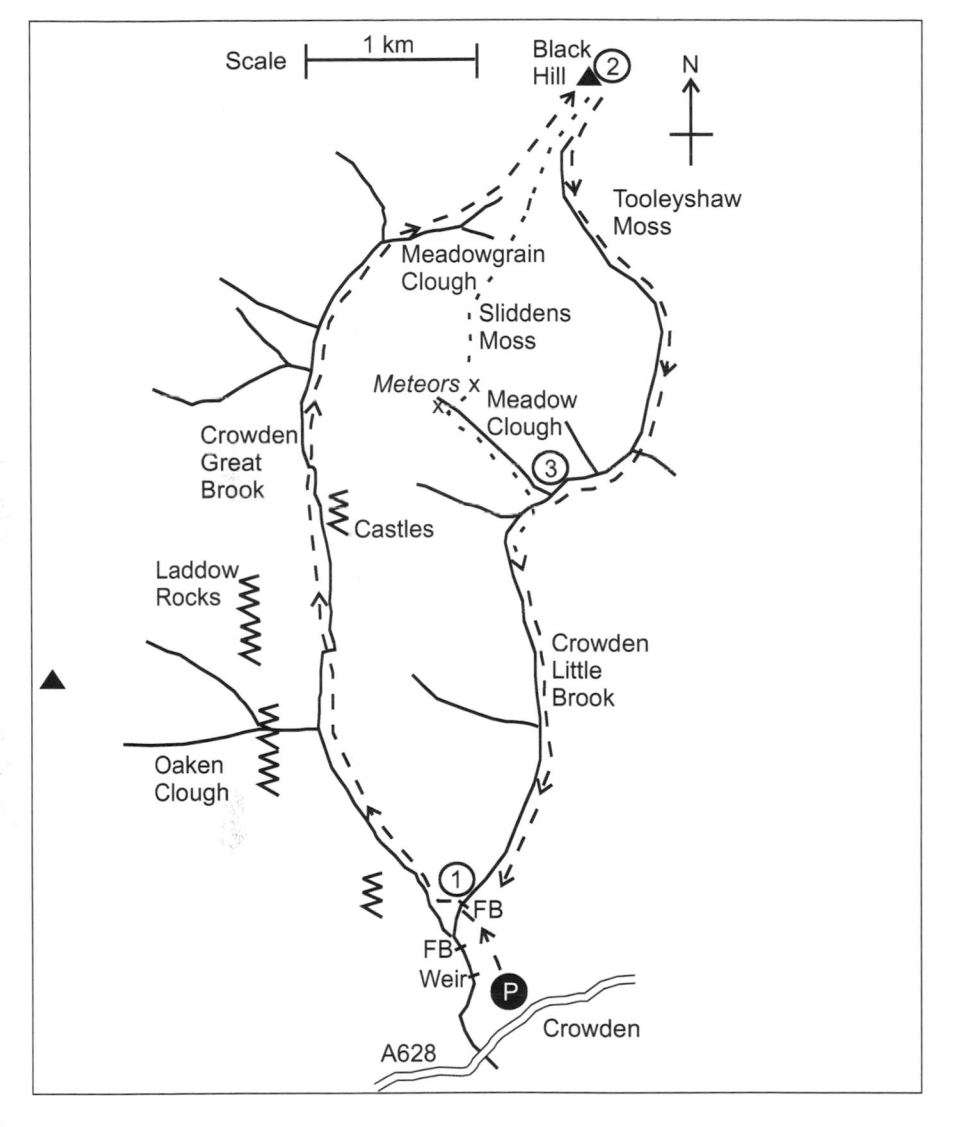

patches to skate across; much easier to walk on than when it's wet underfoot.

Go south and drop down to the start of Crowden Little Brook. There are small waterfalls and cascades. If there isn't too much water, it is possible to walk down the stream bed and climb down the waterfalls. Eventually you return to the confluence you left a few hours earlier. If

Crowden Great Brook from the Castles

you wish to avoid going along Crowden Little Brook there is a path 100m or so to the east of it, which runs above the stream for 2km.

An alternative route from Black Hill is to go on a bearing of 220° for 400m, then south towards Sliddens Moss. There is a thin trail along the top of the moor. Where Meadow Clough peters out, near the top of the moor, there is considerable wreckage from a pair of early jet aircraft, Meteors, which crashed in 1951. Map ref: SE070029 (07037/02906). From the wreckage, follow Meadow Clough down to where it joins Crowden Little Brook (3). There is a lovely 20ft waterfall just before the junction.

# Walk 18. Withens Edge and above the Woodhead Tunnels

**Grade:** Moderate

**Distance:** 15km (9.5 miles)

**Time:** 5-7 hours

**Starting point/parking:** Car park signposted Winscar Reservoir (SE152020) by the minor road, off the A628 Woodhead Pass, that leads to Dunford Bridge

---

## General description

The walk passes three reservoirs as it climbs over the moor to Snailsden Pike. It goes over open moor to Withens Edge and Dead Edge End. Rough ground is crossed to the line of the disused Woodhead railway tunnels. This is followed back to the start. The terrain is very mixed. There are some good tracks but there are also paths over difficult, boggy ground. The first time I did this walk was alone in February on a day when the cloud was nearly low enough to cover the tunnel entrance. In these conditions this walk is a good navigation exercise.

## Route

From the Winscar Reservoir car park, walk north for 300m to the reservoir that feeds the River Don. Bear right along the dam wall keeping the reservoir on the left. Pass by the Broad Hill car park. This is a popular picnic spot in summer. There are public conveniences here. In fact this whole area is delightful. Down in Dunford Bridge is a large car park with details of the Trans Pennine Trail, which passes through here. In summer 2005, by the reservoir, a man was erecting a tent for the 'Moors for the Future' organization. This was conducting surveys to see what people would like to have done in the Peak District. Also, it was raising awareness about restoration, conservation etc. Looking back, you may see the Woodhead Tunnel entrance, or at least the electricity pylons at its mouth. After Winscar Reservoir the track leads to Harden Reservoir.

The target is Snailsden Reservoir, followed by Snailsden Pike. From the

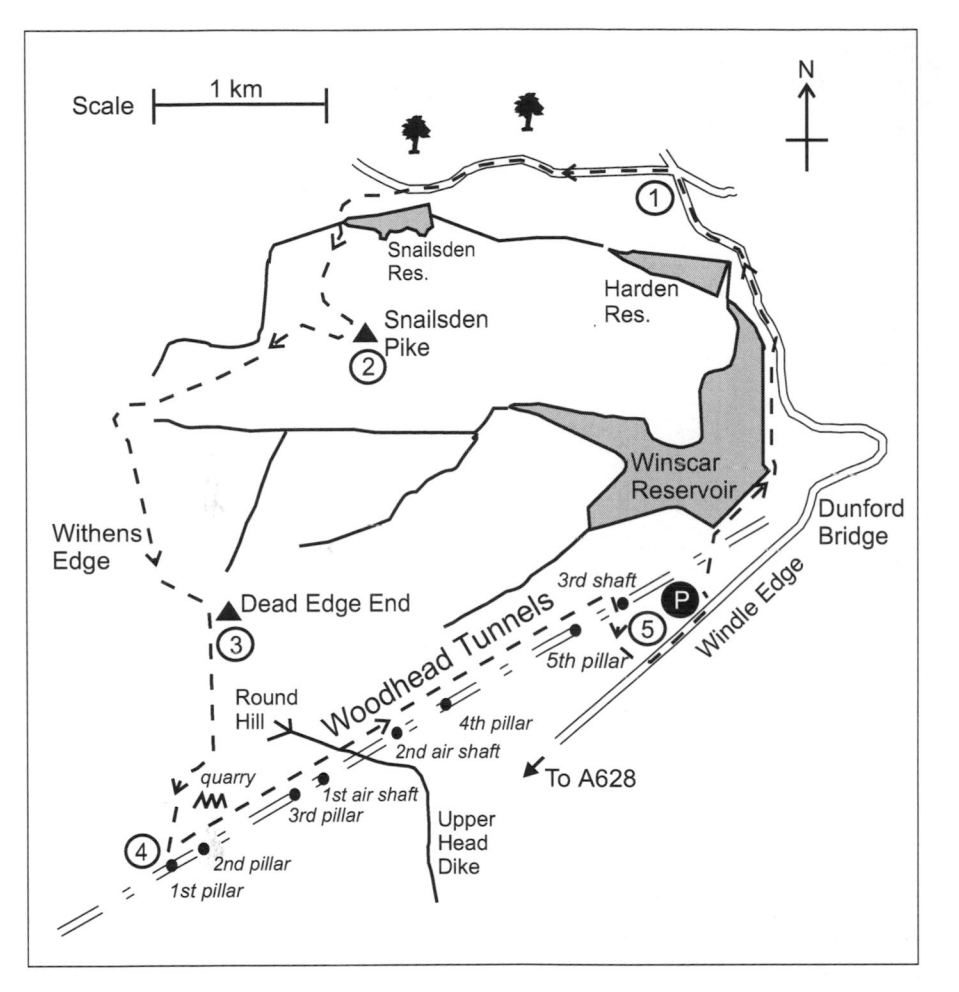

Harden Reservoir Dam, go along the road for 800m to a junction (1), turn left and walk along this road for 1.5km. At SE135041 go through a gate with the open access sign. There is a good track. After 500m take the left fork that goes past the west end of Snailsden Reservoir, then take another left fork. This leads to within 50m of the trig. point on Snailsden Pike, at SE132033 (13200/03315) (2). On a clear day there are lovely views in all directions. Both the Holme Moss and Emley Moor masts may be seen in the distance. On my first walk here, due to cloud, I saw nothing all day. From the trig. point go west, along a thin track, in the direction of the Black Hill mast. At Snailsden Pike End go downhill, then gently uphill, on a bearing of 240°, for 1.5km until the fence along Withens Edge is encountered. Follow this south, then east to the trig. point at Dead End Edge (3). There is a reasonable path on the west side of the fence. Again, there are superb views.

From the trig. point go south for 800m across rough ground to a fence. Turn right and go along the fence to an old stile. Now aim south, to the edge of the moor, crossing a deep grough. Follow the edge to an area of old quarries. There is a good view down the Longdendale valley.

The idea now is to follow the approximate line of the Woodhead tunnels back to Dunford Bridge. The first tunnel was started in 1839 and completed in 1845. A second one was built in 1852 and the third in 1954. They are 3 miles long. Many years ago a colleague was taking part in the Four Inns Walk. He walked down one of the tunnels to avoid heavy rain. Along the line of the tunnels there are various survey pillars and airshafts. Finding them in poor visibility is a good navigation exercise. The first pillar is 300m below the quarries (4). Here, in case it is cloudy, is a list of the features above ground and their 10-figure map references.

| | |
|---|---|
| 1st pillar | SE12140/00326 |
| 2nd pillar | SE12361/00466 |
| 3rd pillar | SE12818/00722 |
| 1st airshaft | SE12972/00808 |
| 2nd airshaft | SE13470/01046 |
| 4th pillar | SE13792/01270 |
| 5th pillar | SE14426/01629 |
| 3rd airshaft | SE14672/01780 |

The direction of the tunnel is 060°

The quarry area is quite extensive. The land between the first and second airshafts is very difficult and following the tunnel line loses height. Alternatively, there is a stile to the north of the first airshaft that leads to level ground, but it is very hard work. Either way is exhausting. On a recent trip I recovered by the square shaped, second shaft and a meadow pipit perched on the wall above and sang its heart out. From this shaft climb the hill, past a brick building. It is good to be on

Woodhead tunnels

the open moor again. At the 4th pillar a good track comes in from the left. This is a well-deserved bonus. It leads to the 3rd shaft (5). The wall is low so it is possible to climb up a few feet and look down the shaft. From the airshaft the car park may be seen, tantalizingly close. However don't make my mistake of going directly to it, even though there is an access gate at the bottom. The tussocks made this the worst ground of the day. Follow the track from the shaft southwards to the minor road and down to the car park. There is a fine picnic table to sit at, and recover, with your boots off.

# Walk 19. West of Black Hill

**Grade:** Moderate

**Distance:** 15km (9.5 miles)

**Time:** 5-7 hours

**Starting point/parking:** Car park off A635, Mossley to Holmfirth road, just past the turn to Dovestone Reservoir (SE018045)

## General description

Holme Clough is used for the start of the route to Black Hill. Birchen Clough is for the way back. There are paths by the sides of the reservoirs at the start and end of this walk but much of it is across open moorland. It is possible to do some scrambling along the stream beds. In cloud the trig. point at the top of Black Hill used to be difficult to find, but now the paving flags lead you there. I did this walk in December with Brian, Dave, Malc and Robin.

## Route

Take the path, out of the car park, that joins the access road down to Yeoman Hey Reservoir. Walk along the west side of the reservoir up to Greenfield Reservoir. Keep to the north of the water and then follow Greenfield Brook to its junction with Birchen Clough at SE038050 (1). Grey wagtails and dippers may be seen here. Take the left fork keeping to the right of the water. This is Holme Clough and is very attractive.

In good conditions there is the possibility of a bit of easy scrambling. Traverse right under the first 8ft waterfall. Another traverse follows on the right side of the stream, to reach the second short waterfall. This can be climbed by slimy rocks on the right, or on good holds on the left. After 300m follow the right fork of the stream. Rimmon Pit Clough is the left fork. On that December day, we had to scramble along the side of the stream, which had a good flow of water, on slippery rocks. At one point Brian hesitated, lunged forward, lost his footing and sat down, up to his chest in icy water. He hauled himself out and succinctly said "car keys". When the flow of water isn't too great the bed of the stream provides a good way up for over 1km.

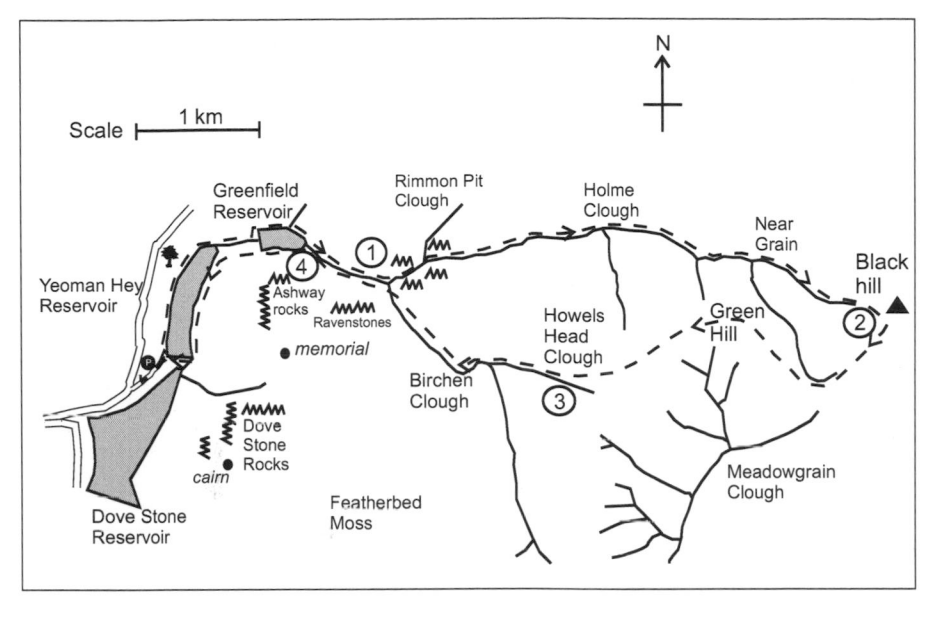

Carry on east beside the clough as it curves its way to Black Hill. It is possible to avoid all the twists and turns of the stream, and aim directly for the top, along a faint track that starts where Holme Clough begins to peter out. On the map the clough is named Near Grain as it gets closer to Black Hill. It cuts deeply into the steep slope that leads to the summit plateau. At the top of the slope go 300m SE to the trig. point (2).

To return, leave the trig. point and aim due west to pass over Green Hill. Keep heading west and avoid any of the cloughs that lead north, unless you wish to return to Holme Clough. 3km from Black Hill the ground slopes down. Follow any of the cloughs that feed into Howels Head Clough (3). This leads to Birchen Clough, which is a fine way down. On that winter's day there was too much water and the rock was too slippery to use the stream bed, so we used the path on the NE side. In good conditions it is possible to enjoy a little scrambling.

Above Greenfield Reservoir there are remains of substantial old walls and a large, foreboding tunnel belonging to the Water Board. This is to let water flow directly from the upper part of Greenfield Brook into the lower reservoir when there is heavy rain. Retrace your earlier steps past Greenfield Reservoir (4). This time, cross to the south side of

Holme Clough

the stream and take a path above the east edge of Yeoman Hey Reservoir. As you reach this dam wall there is a seat that gives a lovely view over Dove Stone Reservoir and this is a good place to finish off any supplies. Cross the dam to return to the car park. Note the plaque on the west end of the dam wall commemorating the King of Tonga's visit in 1981.

When we got back to the car, there was no sign of Brian although there was evidence that he had been back. A man, whose dog had been injured by a car, asked for a lift for the dog and himself but, unfortunately, without the keys we were immobilized. He soon managed to find a helpful motorist. Eventually Brian returned from his stroll down the valley and we headed for the nearest pub. Malc's designs on a large Yorkshire pudding were thwarted as we had just missed the last orders for food. He had to suffer watching a large party devour the various courses of a Christmas dinner. His expression said everything.

# Walk 20. Challenging Crowden Cloughs

**Grade:** Strenuous

**Distance:** 14km (9 miles)

**Time:** 5-7 hours

**Starting point/parking:** Crowden car park by A628 Woodhead Pass (SK072993)

## General Description

This is a circular walk on the moorland north of Crowden, mainly off paths, on boggy ground and along stream beds. Although the distance is not great, the going is tiring and involves ascending and descending several cloughs. There is good scrambling to be had in some of the cloughs.

## Route

From Crowden car park, walk back up the road to the Youth Hostel. On the east side of the hostel there is a signpost and a stile. Go over it and follow a path, above the road, for 800m. A cobbled track leading to the old quarries is met. Take this uphill to a broken wall (SK080997). Turn right, aiming for a small plantation. Climb steps in a wall to enter the field next to the plantation. Cross the field and go up diagonally, through the wood to a good track. This leads to an old building. Don't go through the gate just past the building, but go over a stile round the back of it.

Climb diagonally right across a field. There are two marker posts that indicate the direction. Go through bracken, to a stile in the top right-hand corner above the Hey Clough. The aim is to use this clough to ascend onto the moor. The going is not easy. Use the stream bed as much as possible, as the land each side of it is very tussocky. Step over a fence, just to the right of the clough (1) (my old map shows an access point here but it is now fenced). Go up the clough for 600m, from the fence, to 082007. Leave it here and walk 200m west to a path. Follow this towards White Low. It joins the main path from

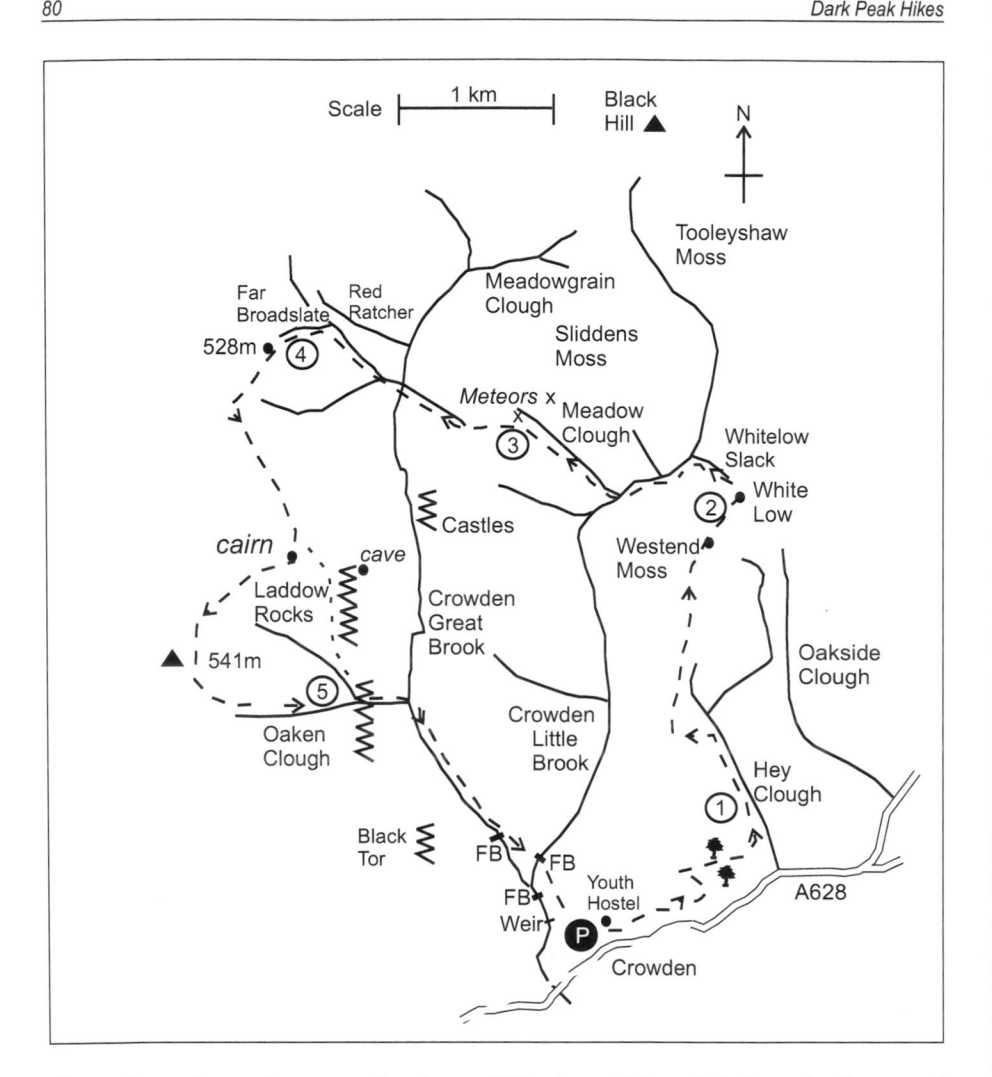

Crowden at a cairn, near the top of Westend Moss. Walk up to the post at White Low (2).

From here, go NW to the start of a clough named Whitelow Slack. There are grouse butts along this clough and there is a land rover track on the right-hand side (a bonus!). Take this to the bottom of the clough, finishing on the left by Crowden Little Brook. Follow this downstream for 600m to the bottom of Meadow Clough (SE074023). Go along this and within a few metres there is a 20ft waterfall. This is too

Meteor wreckage

slimy to climb so bypass it on the left. Next, two more waterfalls are encountered. Go to the left, wider fall. In summer, I managed to climb up its left side on mossy steps. Walk by the side of the clough above this fall, heading NW up the moor. At the top, on Sliddens Moss at SE070029 (07037/02906) there is wreckage of two jet aircraft, both Meteors (3). It is spread over a wide area. Now descend to the west and follow a small clough to Crowden Great Brook (SE062030). Go directly across this and the Pennine Way. Follow the stream that goes NW between Red Ratcher and Far Broadslate. After 400m take the left fork up a stream onto Far Broadslate. The last part is particularly peaty! You should now be on the ridge between Chew Reservoir and the Crowden valley. This is marked at 528m on the map (4).

Keeping on the high ground, go 300m SW, then 1km SE. Black Chew Head, at 1778ft or 542m, is the highest point in Greater Manchester. Find a cairn, 200m to the south, at SE056018 and swing SW, across Laddow Moss and the path to Chew Reservoir, to the next target, which is the trig. point at 046012. Alternatively, simply head for nearby Laddow Rocks and inspect the cave at the northern end.

From here turn due east and follow any grough. They all lead into

Oaken Clough. This is the route down, and is a hidden gem. Some of the bed has green moss on it but most of it is clean rock. One early, 12ft waterfall is bypassed and then the P.W. is crossed (5). The stream is now named Oakenclough Brook. After this it becomes more interesting. First there are several steps, then a 10ft drop that can be climbed down on the right. However, at the bottom is a deep pool. The only escape is via a submerged rock. Next, two large boulders are jammed across the clough. Go past the one on the right, by its right side. Then, either climb down the middle or better still go through a hole on the left. This enters a mossy cave under one of the boulders. Continue down more mossy steps. There is one more problem where it is possible to slide down, on the left, for six feet. I think that this descent is the best part of the walk.

Now follow Crowden Great Brook back to Crowden. There is path on the left bank. Go past a footbridge, taking the path on the left. Look for a path that branches right to a footbridge over Crowden Little Brook. Turn right back to the car park. The campsite shop may be open. If it is, the ice-cream sign is very tempting.

# Walk 21. Chew Reservoir from Arnfield

**Grade:** Strenuous

**Distance:** 16km (10 miles)

**Time:** 5-7 hours

**Starting point/parking:** On a minor road, by Arnfield Reservoir, at its junction with the A628 Woodhead Pass (016973)

## General description

Arnfield Reservoir is one of the closest points to Stockport for access to the moors. This walk uses the path to Lad's Leap then goes north to Chew Reservoir. The return is along Hoarstone Edge and down to the Swineshaw Reservoirs. Much of the going is pathless and boggy. The return may be shortened, by using the path above Ogden Clough. In clouds finding the trig. point south of Chew Reservoir can provide good compass practice. The sites of several wartime aircraft wrecks are visited.

## Route

Walk up the lane, away from the main road, and turn left at the top. After another 400m, before dropping down to a bridge, take the sign-posted footpath on the right (1). Follow this, south of Arnfield Brook, for 2km. It rises gradually to a small, disused reservoir. There is an old pipe-line coming out of it, heading in the direction of Tintwistle. The path continues up the hill. Below, to the right, an area of land is fenced off. There is a path leading down to the A628. For those willing to make a small diversion, there is a plaque to the memory of the crews of the aircraft that crashed nearby. The plaque is attached to the fence 300m down the path. In 1945 three Hurricanes crashed into the hill-side. There is a small cairn with minute amounts of wreckage, inside the fenced area at SK035988 (03562/98890).

Back above the fence line, follow the path up the slope. There are two other sites of aircraft wrecks in the vicinity. One is that of a Lancaster bomber near the top of Tintwistle Knarr. It crashed in 1948. To find it, you need to leave the path and go north along a track towards the top

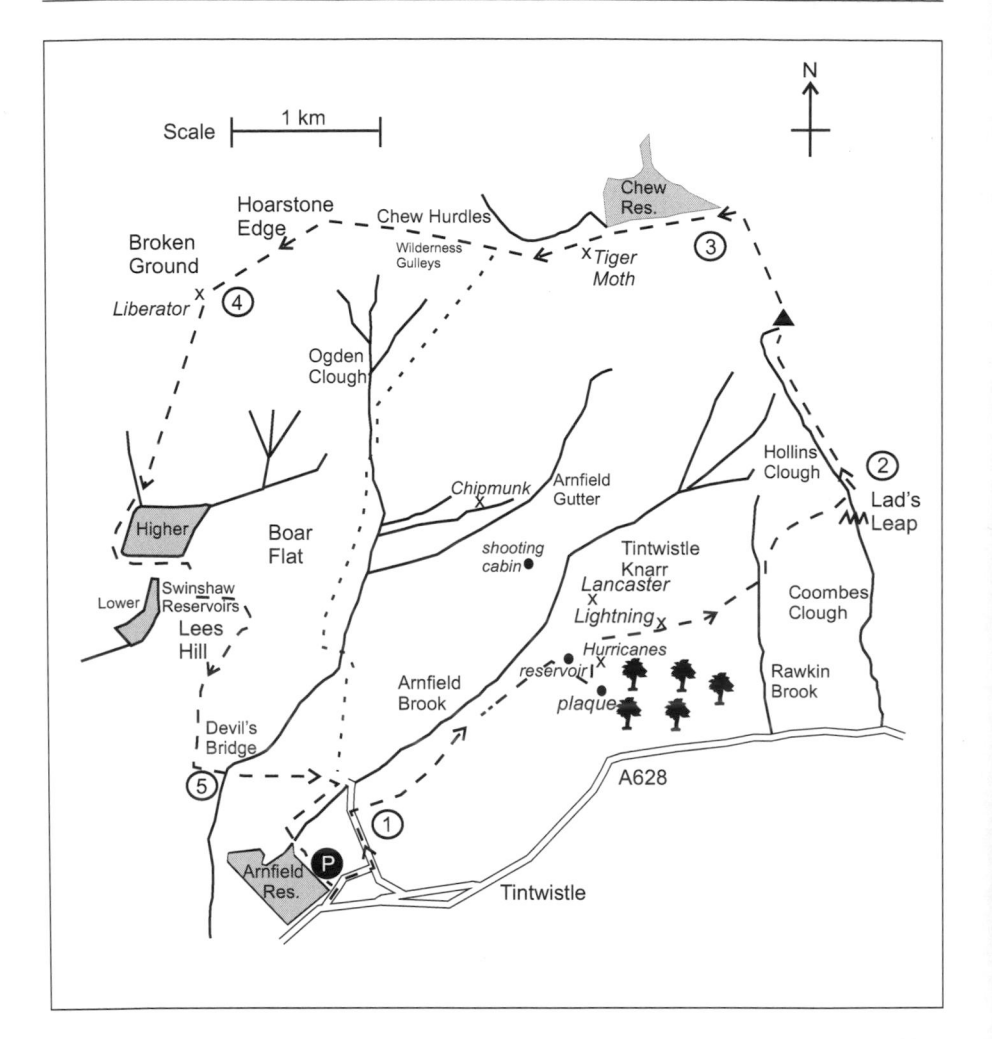

of Tintwistle Knarr. The wreckage is in a wide gulley that starts on the west side of a stile and fence. The wreckage is 100m down the gulley in the direction of Arnfield Reservoir. Map ref: SK035992 (03563/99263). If you find a set of car keys in the area, they are mine. I had to catch two buses home to get the spare keys.

The other site is back, near the path to Lad's Leap. It is that of an American Lightning that crashed in 1944. This is 400m along the path to Lad's Leap from the corner of the fenced-off land. It is marked by a post, 40m to the north of the path. Map ref: SK039990 (03926/99084).

Chew reservoir

The aforementioned plaque is to the crews of the Hurricanes and the Lightning.

One further item of interest may be found in this area. On several occasions I have seen a flock of small birds here. I'm told they may be twite. Twice I have seen sparrow-hawks. It doesn't take too much imagination to see why they were around.

After all this excitement, carry on along the muddy path towards Lad's Leap. By a stile, the path leaves the fence and goes up towards Lad's Leap. (It is possible to keep east until Coombes Clough is reached and use that to scramble up the hill.) At Lad's Leap leave the path – it's no great loss (2).

Follow the clough (now named Hollins Clough) into the heart of the moor. Have fun, particularly in cloud, trying to navigate for 1.5km to the trig. point at SE046012. Having found the trig. point head north 800m to Chew Reservoir (or the path which leads east from it) (3). Go west along the south side of the reservoir to the dam. Take the path that leads just south of west, on the southern edge of the valley. There is a small amount of wreckage of a Tiger Moth 300m from the reservoir, and 100m south of the path (see Walk 15).

Carry on along the path until a cairn and post are reached near Chew Hurdles, at 027015. En route, two gulleys, East and West Wilderness Gulleys, are passed. It was here that two climbers died in an avalanche in 1963. The gulleys can provide a scramble route into or out of the valley below.

A path leads SW from the post to Ogden Clough and follows it back to Arnfield reservoir. Ogden Clough, itself, provides a boggy route to Arnfield. I have disturbed snipe on a couple of occasions when I have followed the stream.

If you can face more rough ground, the route goes due west from Chew Hurdles, over desolate moor for 2km. At SE008012 (00875/01203) and SE 008016 (00808/01643), on Broken Ground is wreckage of a Liberator aircraft (4). What little there is, is spread over a wide area. The American four-engine bomber ran out of fuel. The eleven personnel on board parachuted to safety over Lincolnshire, leaving the plane to crash in the Peak District. This was in 1943. From this spot there are good views down to the area south of Mossley.

Now go southwards for 1.5km to Upper Swineshaw Reservoir. Walk along the west side and go across the dam wall. Take the path heading east, then skirt round Lees Hill (or, for a good view, go over it), and go south on a path to a junction. Turn east and walk to Devil's Bridge (5) – there are various alternative paths here. Head east to the farm at Arnfield. Instead of taking the lane you came out on, take the path signposted on the right, through a nature reserve. After 400m turn left to go along the NE side of Arnfield Reservoir, back to the lane from where you started.

Note: The crash site of a Chipmunk aircraft, from 1951, is near Arnfield Gutter. The pilot survived. Map ref: SE027998 (02733/99872).

# Section 4: The Eastern Moors

This area is to the east of the Derwent valley and links up with the Bleaklow region. Margery Hill is the highest point of South Yorkshire at 1791ft or 546m. There is a long ridge above the Derwent and Howden Reservoirs. The west edge of the ridge has interesting outcrops and rocks; the east has sloping moors. Much of the ground is boggy or covered with heather.

There is a path along the ridge, named Howden Edge, which leads towards Bleaklow Stones. Cut Gate links the top of Howden Reservoir with Langsett. There is also a path from Howden Reservoir to Alport Castles. Another path goes north from the top of Howden Reservoir along the River Derwent.

Three of the walks are to Margery Hill. One walk is to Back Tor from Bradfield. The remaining walk visits Bamford Edge (only recently open access) and the Stanage area. Note: all the map references in this section have the prefix SK, unless otherwise stated.

Margery Hill trig point

# Walk 22. Margery Hill from Howden Reservoir

**Grade:** Easy

**Distance:** 14km (9 miles)

**Time:** 4-6 hours

**Starting point/parking:** At the end of road by Howden Reservoir (Mon-Fri) (167939). Sat & Sun park at Fairholmes Centre and catch the minibus to end of road

## General description

The walk starts along Howden reservoir and the River Derwent. There is a short ascent to Outer Edge. Howden Edge is followed past Margery Hill. The descent is by Howden Clough. Much of this is on paths, apart from short sections when ascending and descending the moor. The remains of two aircraft are visited. Also the crater caused by a V1 is close to the route. Another wreck requires a long walk across heather to reach it. From along Howden Edge there are excellent views to the west.

## Route

Go north from the end of the tarmac road for just over 1km, along a good track, to the footbridge over the River Derwent at Slippery Stones. The bridge was reconstructed here after the dams were built and the valley was flooded. Cross the bridge, and keep on the track which follows the main valley north. Walk north for 1km until there is a fork in the path (1). Take the right fork that rises gradually and leads to Broadhead Clough.

A trail goes part of the way up this clough. However, halfway up, strike NE looking for the easiest way through the heather and undergrowth to the top, where there are some large boulders. In May we saw half a dozen mountain hares on these slopes, by then mainly back in their brown coats. 200m along the edge to the NW, there is a series of grouse butts. By one of the lower butts, in a clough, there is

Outer Edge

wreckage of a civilian aircraft, a Consul. It crashed in 1951. Map ref: 174966 (17407/96628).

A thin path leads past the butts onto the moor. Take this, then aim NE to the trig. point at Outer Edge (2). There are lovely views across the valley towards Grinah and Barrow Stones.

From Outer Edge turn SE and follow a boggy path for about 500m. To the left, east of the path, there are a few remnants of an Oxford, a trainer aircraft, from 1943. Map ref: 180967 (18025/96710). The main bits are 20m east of the path. A few more molten bits of metal are just a metre or two off the path.

The next target is the trig. point on Margery Hill. But, 700m from the Oxford site on a bearing of 110°, is the site where a V1 is supposed to have exploded. Map ref: 185965 (18566/96507). There isn't actually a crater now, more of a muddy, bare patch that is often under water. It is 15m in circumference with a few tufts of grass here and there. When I was there a couple of years ago there was a piece of metal, about 40cm by 20cm, which may have been part of the V1, in the centre of

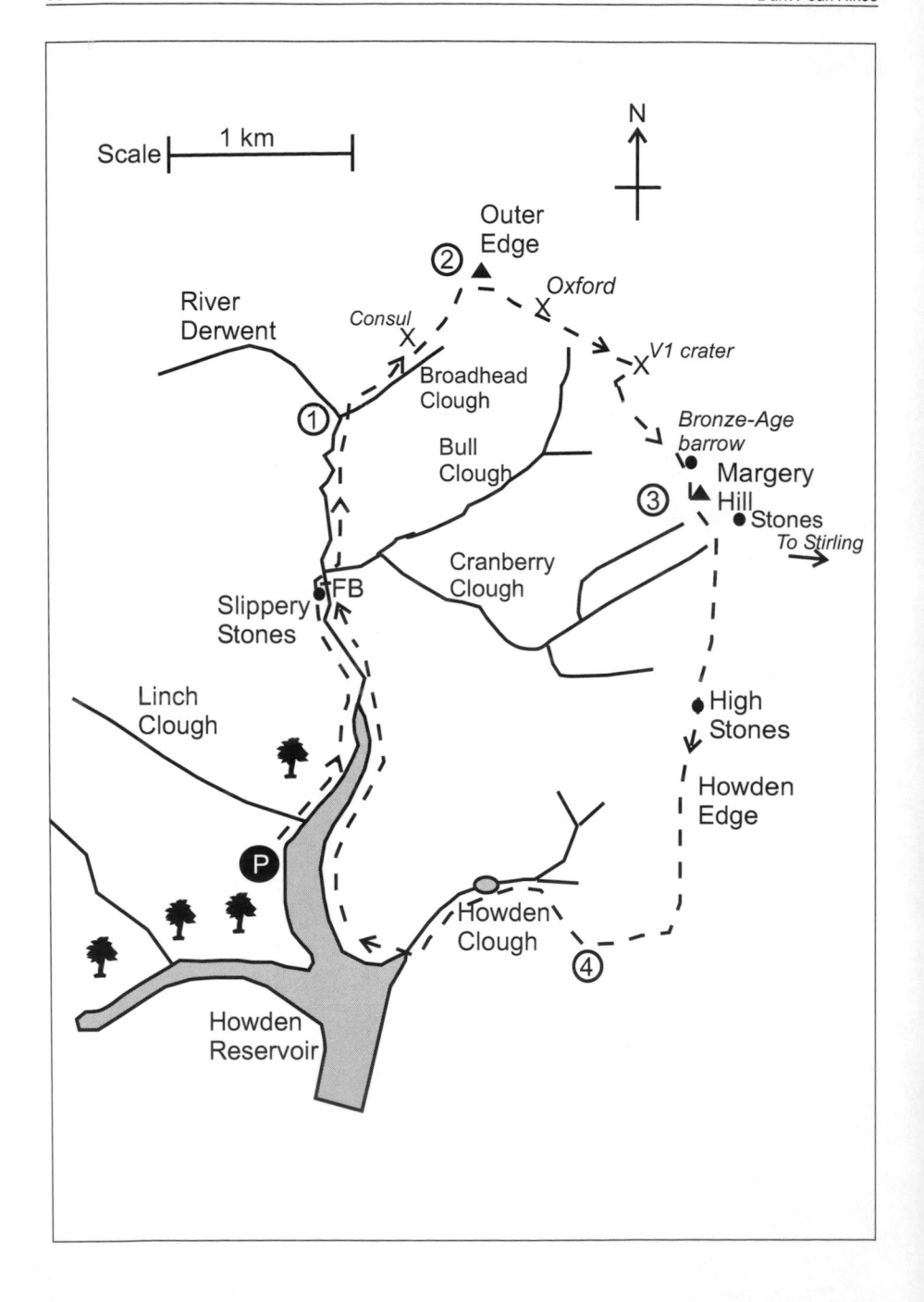

Scale ⊢━━━ 1 km ━━━⊣

N

**River
Derwent**

**Outer
Edge**

②  ▲

*Oxford*
X

*Consul*
X

*V1 crater*
X

**Broadhead
Clough**

①

**Bull
Clough**

*Bronze-Age
barrow*
●

▲  **Margery
Hill**

③

● **Stones**

*To Stirling*
→

**Cranberry
Clough**

**Slippery
Stones**

●FB

● **High
Stones**

**Linch
Clough**

🌳

**Howden
Edge**

P

🌳  🌳

🌳

**Howden
Clough**

④

**Howden
Reservoir**

this area. The last time I visited it had disappeared. If you're wondering how a V1 had the range to get this far, the answer is that they were slung under Heinkel bombers and launched from over the North Sea. Over 20 V1's landed in the north of England.

Around this area in May, we saw two dunlin. At that time of year they would be nesting. Also, in contrast to the hares we saw earlier, there was one with a much whiter coat.

Return to the path and continue towards Margery Hill. A trench containing a path, Cut Gate, is crossed by a cairn. The trig. point on Margery Hill is 500m from this junction. Just before the top, an area has been fenced-off. Inside is a 3500 year-old Bronze-Age barrow. There are some large rocks close to the trig. point that give good shelter if there is a cold wind (3). Now follow the path south, for just over 1km, to High Stones.

There is the opportunity to divert to the crash site of a Stirling bomber (this adds 2.5 km to the walk). It crashed on Upper Commons in 1944. The good news is that all ten of the crew survived. The bearing from Margery Hill is 095°. There is a faint path to start with but this peters out. The way down to it is through heather and over groughs. Curlews nest on the moor, making their liquid, haunting calls. Occasional tracks and burnt patches of heather make progress slightly easier. The wreckage is spread over quite a large area. Map ref: 201955 (20157/95524). A large cabin is visible in the distance, and an outcrop of rocks is to the right. Since a previous visit, a couple of years ago, some of the larger pieces have been removed.

From the wreckage make your way back west towards the main path, or aim directly over groughs, to High Stones.

From High Stones, where there are fine views of the Kinder plateau in the distance, follow a good track south along Howden Edge for 1km.

Views of Lose Hill and Back Tor come into sight. Height is lost gradually. The wide track turns west and drops down to a gate at a flat area (4). A path makes its way ahead but leave this after 200m, heading NW across difficult terrain to Howden Clough. Here we saw another curlew. (Note: the main track will take you to the bottom of Abbey Brook but this lengthens the walk.) There is a path on the other side of the stream in Howden Clough. When we were there in May, a pair of

Canada Geese and their three offspring occupied the small reservoir. Follow the path down through a wood and join the main path round Howden Reservoir. Turn right and walk along this path, for over 2km, back to the pack-horse bridge at Slippery Stones. It is just over 1km back to the parking area.

# Walk 23. Margery Hill by Abbey Brook

**Grade:** Moderate

**Distance:** 18km (11 miles)

**Time:** 5-7 hours

**Starting point/parking:** At the end of road by Howden Reservoir (Monday to Friday) (167939). Sat & Sun park at Fairholmes Centre and catch the minibus to end of road.

## General description

An easy start along Howden reservoir is followed by a pleasant ascent by Abbey Brook. The walk continues along the ridge to Margery Hill. The descent is by either Cut Gate or Cranberry Clough. The last time I did this walk was on a summer's day in July with two friends who used paths rather than the streams for ascent and descent.

## Route

From the end of the tarmac road, go north for 1.5km along the track to the bridge at Slippery Stones (1). Cross over, and go left for 100m to pick up the track which doubles back along Howden Reservoir. This is a nice stroll for 3km, passing the Howden Reservoir dam. Look out for goshawks in spring and summer. I've yet to see one though I'm told this is a good place, but we did see a blackcap.

500m after the dam, take the path signposted Ewden via Broomhead (2). Follow this through the wood for 200m to a gate. The main track swings uphill heading for Strines. Keep left, on the track above the trees. After a further 300m go through another gate. The idea is to drop down the heather slope on the left to Abbey Brook. There is a broken wall to step over. Try to pick a way down through the undergrowth. This is the worst part of the walk. My companions Brian and Peter opted to stay on the path above Abbey Brook all the way to the top of the moor.

Once the brook is reached the going is relatively easy. There is a sheep track on the right bank that goes through alder trees and patches of bracken. At a steep bank on the right, switch sides for 50m.

Abbey Brook

The way goes past some lovely pools and the constant babbling of the brook keeps one company. At 190928 the trees peter out. The stream bed may be used occasionally. After a further 600m, a 12ft slimy water slide is best bypassed, on either side. I didn't fancy my chances of scaling it directly. 50m past here take the left fork. The right fork is Sheepfold Clough. Dippers may be seen along the stream.

Using either one of the banks or the stream bed, carry on up the valley. There are no difficulties and the surroundings are wonderful (on a summer's day!). Take the left fork when Bents Clough joins on the right. The rocky steps give reasonably good footing. A narrow gorge can be climbed through on the left. A nice pool, with a 6ft water slide on the right, is reached. Here I slipped and my left leg got immersed up to the thigh. A grey wagtail was hopping around the rocks above the pool.

At 200927 take the right fork, as Crook Clough comes in on the left. An 8ft waterfall is reached. The water comes down on the right, but the slimy rocks on the left can be climbed, using a good handhold for a pull up. Just above here the bed flattens out, so leave it to join the path, which is close by, on the right-hand side. I caught up with my two

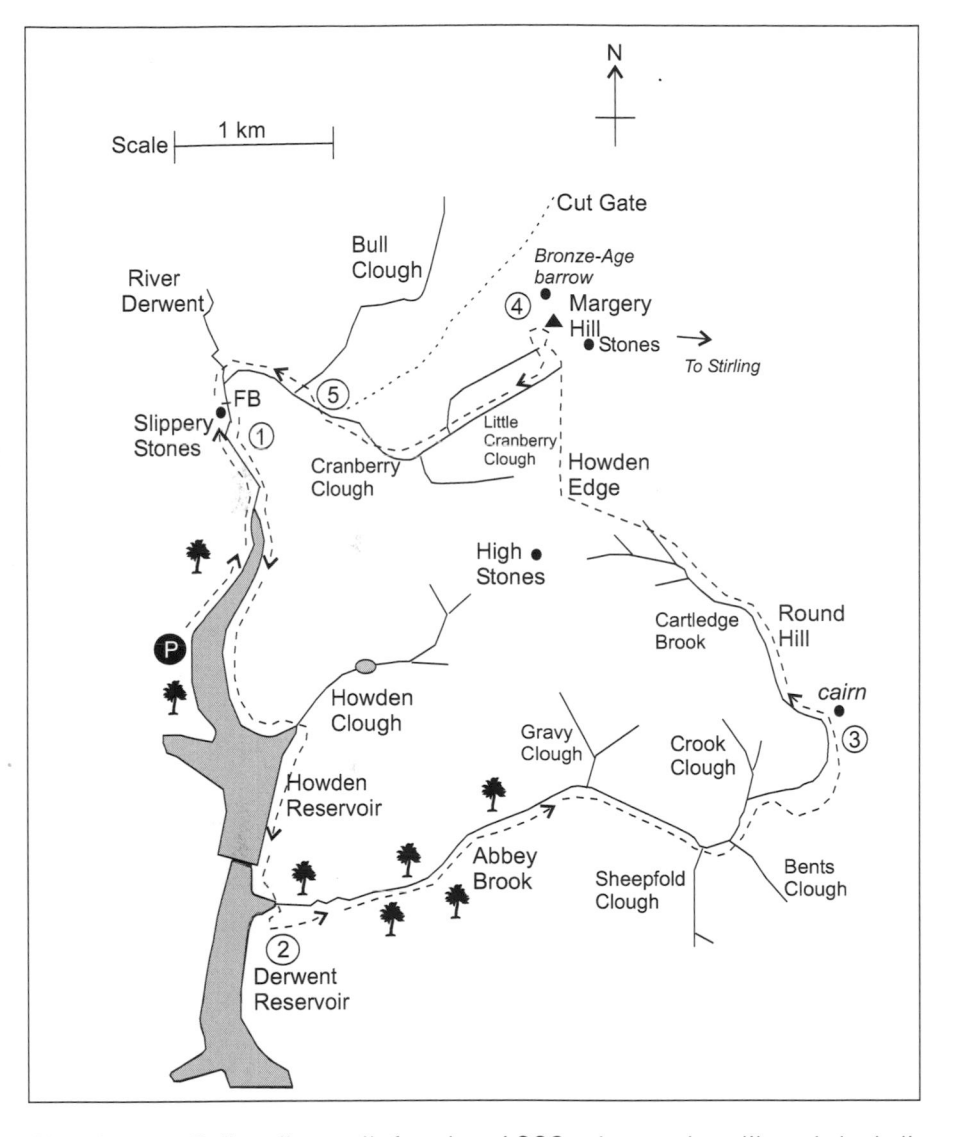

friends here. Follow the path for about 800m to a cairn with a stake in it. A stone pillar bears the initials RRW. Map ref: 207934 (20769/93415) (3).

The path forks here with the main path going on to Broomhead Moor. Take the left branch on a bearing of 330° towards Round Hill. In good conditions this is a good path, although it isn't marked on the map. It keeps close to Cartledge Brook passing grouse butts, then swings more towards the west on a bearing of 300°. Here are a few map references along it, to help if it is cloudy and you lose the path. 196942 (19659/94218); 194944 (19408/94491); and 188954 (18869 95408) (the last one is where the path meets Howden Edge). Now continue north on a good path for 1km. The trig. point at Margery Hill is 250m from the edge (4). The mast at Emley Moor and a wind farm can be seen to the NE.

From here there is a choice of routes down. The easy way is to continue on the path for 500 m to Cut Gate and turning left, take this down to Slippery Stones. On the way to Cut Gate there is a 3500 year-old barrow from the Bronze Age that has been fenced off for research. Alternatively, go south along the edge from Margery Hill for 300m. Then drop down the moor alongside Little Cranberry Clough. The going is difficult over tussocky ground. Follow the clough down, the way eases, but not a lot. The bed can help a bit but this isn't a very pleasant route, although there is nice scenery. I don't really recommend this clough but I have been along it a couple of times. About 1km from the start of the Cranberry Clough you join Cut Gate (5).

While I waited for my companions, I met two people carrying out a survey. They were from Trent & Nottingham University and were taking water samples as part of a project about the management and sustainability of the water supply. They mentioned that further work was being done in the River Ashop area, on Featherbed Moss. A couple of grey wagtails sang in a tree on the bank.

From here it's only 500m back to Slippery Stones and a stroll back to the car parking area.

# Walk 24. Back Tor and Emlin from Low Bradfield

**Grade:** Moderate

**Distance:** 18km (11 miles)

**Time:** 5-7 hours

**Starting point/parking:** Car park down a lane, The Sands, by Low Bradfield cricket ground (west side) (262920)

## General description

The walk starts along Dale Dike and Strines Reservoirs and climbs up to Back Tor above the Derwent Valley. It goes north along Derwent Edge. There is a choice of routes back, either over a heather moor to Emlin or by Dukes Road across Broomhead Moor (this adds 2km). Good paths are used for most of this walk. The route to Emlin involves two miles of pathless, heather moor. The site of a wartime aircraft crash may be visited on Broomhead Moor

I first did this walk on a dank, cloudy, winter's day with Chris, Pete and Gary from The Byron in Sheffield. The intention was to return by the Duke's Road but due to lack of concentration we ended up on the moor leading to Emlin. We escaped north from the ridge over atrocious ground to Agden Bridge. I repeated the route on a pleasant summer's day, this time heading south from Emlin on a good track.

## Route

Go back along The Sands, turn right and follow the minor road west (this is north of Dale Dike). Go straight on at a junction after 200m. At Annet Bridge take the right fork, following a signpost to Midhopestones & Penistone. Just over 1.5km from the start of the walk, take a footpath on the left at a sign 'Dale Dike Reservoir' (1). Follow this for 400m to the dam wall (ignore a footpath to the left). The first dam was built in 1864 but on March 11th, as it was being filled, it gave way, causing a flood that killed 244 people. It was rebuilt in 1875. There is a memorial plaque and an information board by the path. Go through two stiles, 20m apart, to a path along the NW bank of the reservoir.

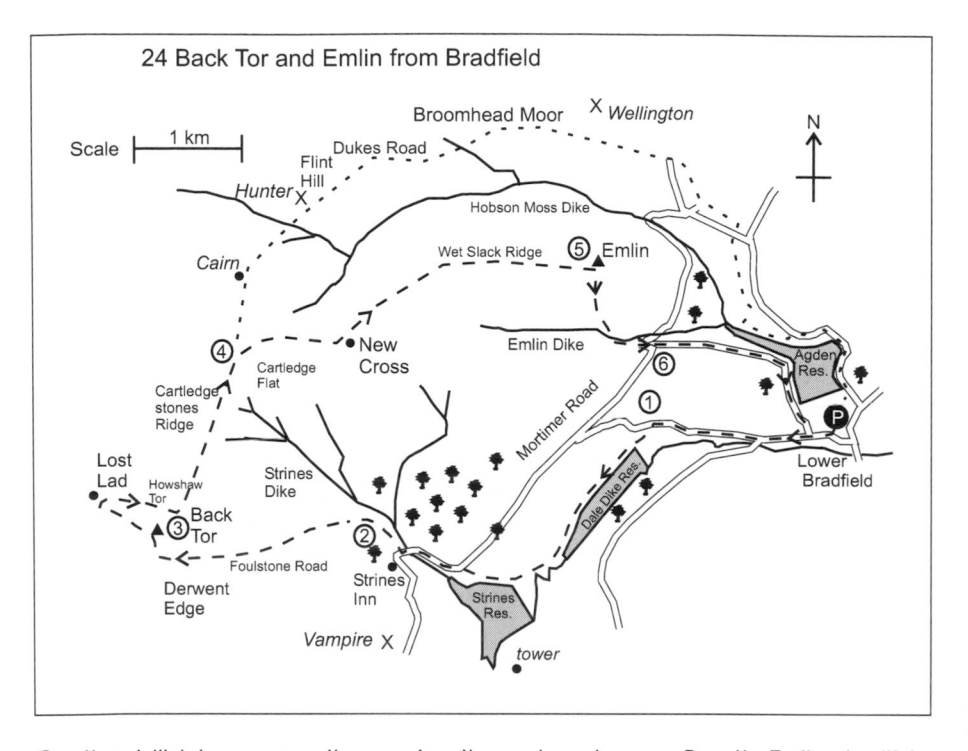

24 Back Tor and Emlin from Bradfield

On the hillside across the water there is a tower, Boot's Folly, built in 1926-7, for Mr. Charles Boot, to provide employment. At the end of the reservoir, the path crosses two footbridges in quick succession and climbs up to the dam wall of Strines Reservoir (built in 1871). The path continues to a road. Turn left in the direction of the Strines Inn. After 600m, take the well-marked bridle way through Bole Edge Plantation (2). At a cattle grid, go straight on and leave the tarmac road. This wide track is called Foulstone Road and leads all the way to Derwent Edge. At the edge, go north for 300m to the trig. point at Back Tor (3). The pillar is perched on top of a rocky outcrop and requires a quick scramble up to it.

It is worth taking the path for 500m to the direction finder at Lost Lad. This was erected by the famous Sheffield Clarion Ramblers in honour of W H Baxby, a former member. Then go east, past Howshaw Tor, to pick up the main path that heads roughly north. Follow this for 1.5km along Cartledge Stones Ridge, to a rocky outcrop on a high point at 207927 (20732/92700) (4).

Lost Lad viewpoint

Now, there is the option of a route that is 2km longer but on a path, verses a shorter route that involves 3km of pathless, heather bashing.

Option 1: Continue on the path north for 1km to 207934 (20769/93415) and take Duke's Road, NE across Flint Hill, then east over Broomhead Moor. At 23482/95419 there is a small amount of wreckage from a Wellington bomber that crashed in 1942. This is 600m north of the path, above of a set of grouse butts. The few bits of metal are not easy to find. Duke's Road meets Mortimer Road at 245945. Take the footpath on the opposite side of the road, and turn right almost immediately, over a stile. After 1km, fork right to Agden Side Road. Take the path on the other side of the road. This leads down Agden Reservoir and back to Low Bradfield.

Option 2: Note: there is a sign at the exit from this moor saying 'No Dogs'. At 207927 there is a path, bearing 100°, which goes across the moor towards New Cross. It peters out about 100m before this. There is a stone plinth at 216928 (21613/92870) which presumably once bore a cross. From here go on a bearing of 050° for 800m towards Wet Slack Edge. There is a stone pillar, with the letters RRW at 221933 and another 300m further on with the letters BJY. Now aim east, for just over 1.5km, to the trig. point on the hill named Emlin (5). On a clear summer's day the going isn't too bad. There are swathes of short young heather or burnt patches that make for easier progress. I imagine that trig. point at Emlin is one of the least visited pillars in the Dark Peak. Map ref: 239933 (23989/93369). There are good views of the reservoirs to the east. Go south to pick up a track past grouse butts. This leads to a footbridge, the route marked by two posts with white tops, over Emlin Dike, and down to Mortimer Road next to a Transco gas pipe (244926) (6). Turn left, then immediately right, downhill towards Agden Reservoir. Either follow this quiet road, or take the path on the left, through trees, that leads to the side of the reservoir. 400m after the dam wall turn left and back to the car park by the cricket ground.

Updates:

Wreckage of a Hunter that crashed in 1993 lies between Round Hill and Flint Hill about 400m NW of Dukes Road at SK208943 (20851/94345).

Also, on Strines Moor a small amount of molten metal from a Vampire that crash-landed in 1951, the pilot survived, lies 700m south of the Strines Inn and 200m west of the road at SK218898 (21844/89801).

# Walk 25. Stanage and Bamford Edge

**Grade:** Strenuous

**Distance:** 19km (12.5 miles)

**Time:** 6-8 hours

**Starting point/parking:** By the top of Redmires Reservoirs (256855)

## General description

Due to the 'right to roam' act Bamford Edge is now open access. The walk combines this with the moorland around Stanage Edge. Parts of the walk are on good paths but where it goes across open moorland the going can be very difficult, particularly after a spell of wet weather. It is advisable not to cross these moors in the nesting season. Note: the route described starts from Redmires Reservoirs but, for those people coming from west of the Pennines, several miles of driving can be saved by parking at Cutthroat Bridge on the A57 (Map ref: 213874) and using a good track above Jarvis Clough to join the route.

## Route

Take the signposted footpath near the NW corner of the top reservoir. After 200m turn off left and take one of the tracks leading to the top of the old quarry area (1). A recent TV documentary described how, in training for the First World War, the Sheffield Pals practised digging trenches on the moors near Sheffield. The view from a helicopter showed marks on the ground made by this digging. There is raised ground that looks like this kind of disturbance. After 90 years it is hard to distinguish these marks unless you can afford a helicopter trip. One line I found is SW of the top of the quarry, 15m above a ruined wall. Map ref: 255858 (25532/85815). There are more lines that appear to zigzag in trench fashion higher up the moor. Map ref: 254858 (25487/85888).

From this bumpy ground, head west through broken walls to the northern edge of Broadshaw Plantation. There is a good track across the fields for a few hundred metres. A wall needs to be crossed at the NW corner of a field. There isn't a stile, but there is a low point near the corner, where it is possible to step over without causing damage. Now

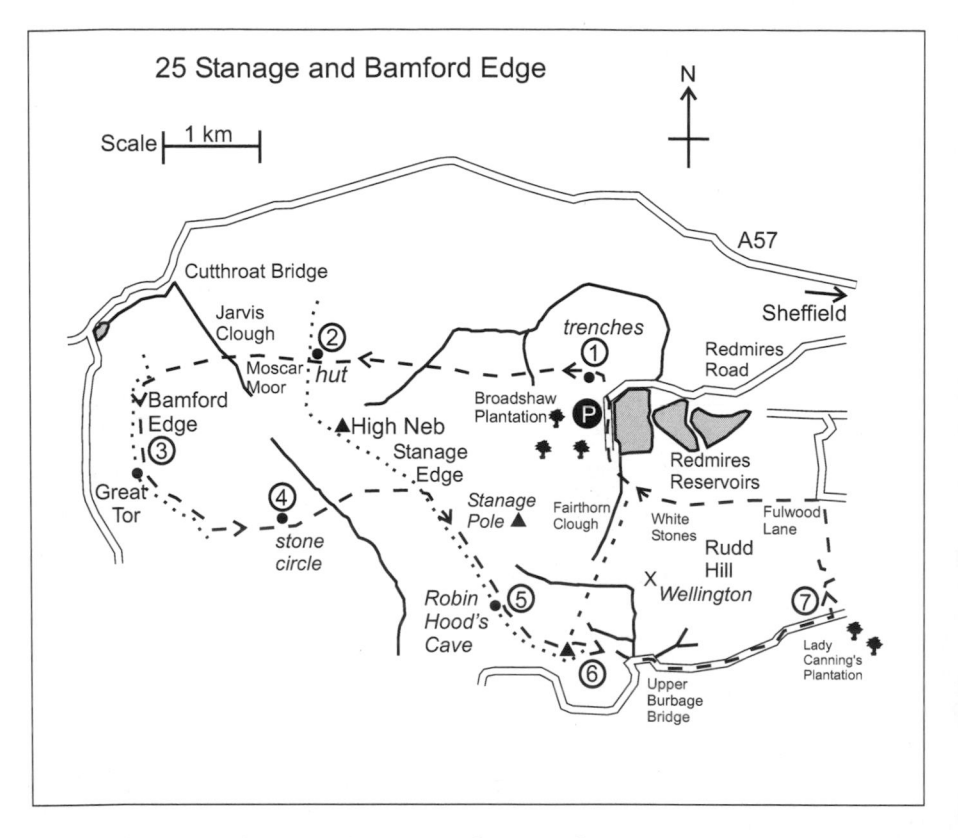

25 Stanage and Bamford Edge

aim just south of a small copse (Oaking Clough Plantation). A white stake gives the direction. Keep aiming roughly west across difficult terrain. This is a fine area for curlew and golden plover. Aim for a ruined hut (Map ref: 226862), which is seen on the horizon on Stanage Edge. This makes a good place for a stop, providing shelter from cold winds (2).

From the Edge you may be able to see Bamford Moor, which is where the route is heading. There is a line of grouse butts/wooden boards below Stanage Edge, across Moscar Moor, leading to the top of Jarvis Clough. Aim for these, a path links them and turns into a wider track. I have seen a pair of ring ouzels here. Go to a hut, by the start of a wall, near the top of Jarvis Clough. Follow the wall across the moor, slightly south of due west. 700m of heathery ground has to be crossed to reach Bamford Edge. This is the shortest way across.

Redmires reservoirs

Take the path that runs south along the Edge past Great Tor (3). There are fine views of Ladybower Reservoir. Beyond the dam is Win Hill and, to the north, is the Derwent valley and its reservoirs. Bamford Edge is a traditional climbing area but was out of bounds until the 'right to roam' act. There are several, awkward looking overhangs. A friend, Chris Hill, tells me that on the several occasions he tried to climb there he was always spotted and asked to leave.

Enjoying the views, carry on along the edge until it starts to peter out. At 212845 leave the Edge and go east across the moor, aiming back to Stanage Edge. A stone circle lies 1km away and just about merits a visit (4). Map ref: 221845 (22118/84533). It is not easy to see unless you are close to it. From the circle, continue across the moor towards the north corner of a wood. By the side of the wood is a wide track up to Stanage Edge. Reaching this track is a major achievement. My route to it was very unpleasant underfoot.

A good track leads up to Stanage Edge and you will feel that you deserve this luxury. Keep on the edge past Robin Hood's Cave (Map ref: 244835 (24443/83580)). Most people will know about this and it makes an ideal place for a stop (5). Continue SE along the edge for 1km to a trig. point (6).

From here take the path, east, to Upper Burbage Bridge and go along the road for 2km, to the edge of Lady Canning's Plantation (7). A path goes north, past Brown Edge Farm, to Fulwood Lane. Turn left along the lane for a few steps then take the path west for 2km to White Stones and past the reservoirs to the end of Redmires Road.

It is possible to cut directly across the moor from the trig. point (6) to the reservoir. I have tried it and cannot recommend it. In nesting and lambing time it should be avoided. After struggling through deep heather you reach tussocks that make you wish you were back in the heather. You then come across bogs that make you yearn for the tussocks. I staggered along the east side of Fairthorn Clough. There were sheep tracks; also sheep bones and skulls that gave an idea of how difficult the sheep find the terrain. Eventually the path from White Stones is met. This goes to the reservoirs.

Update:

Wreckage from a Wellington bomber that crashed in 1942 lies on the moor between Redmires Reservoir and Upper Burbage Bridge at SK261838 (26157/83824). The way to it from any direction is boggy and tussocky.

# Walk 26. Mickleden Beck and Howden Edge

**Grade:** Strenuous

**Distance:** 21km (13 miles); shorter option 15 km (9.5 miles)

**Time:** 6-8 hours

**Starting point/parking:** Car park 400m south of the roundabout, where the A628 and A616 meet, near the Flouch Inn/Hotel (SE201012)

## General description

The walk goes through woods near Langsett Reservoir. It follows Mickleden Beck to Margery Hill and then goes along Howden Edge. Two alternative finishes are given. The shorter one descends to Hordon Clough by a good path. The longer one keeps on Howden Edge to the source of Loftshaw Brook and follows it down to Langsett. Much of the walk is over difficult terrain. After a wet spell the paths will be boggy.

## Route

Take the path at the southern end of the car park. Cross the A616 and enter the wood, by the path opposite the car park gate. On the Sunday we did the walk, the car park was full. There had been an all-night party/rave down by the river. In the wood walk west for 400m, ignoring a signpost to Langsett. Turn left at a signpost 'Bridleway to Derwent'. Go south for 400m and cross a bridge. This is where the 'rave' had taken place. There were still quite a few revellers around. They were friendly and chatty. We were impressed by large hammock-like netting, in a tree, that looked as if it could sleep six. It looked like they'd had a good night and we were rather envious. (Mind you, I can remember attending an event 'The 14-hour Technicolour Dream' at Alexander Palace back in 19**!).

Turn west along The Porter (or Little Don River). Go along either bank, for 1km, to a footbridge. In a further 400m, turn south along Mickleden Beck (189998) (1). This route is long and the terrain tiring but the scenery is excellent.

The Porter (Little Don River)

The stream meanders like a miniature river, in its narrow valley. There are sheep tracks but you have to cross the beck repeatedly. This first stretch is lovely. Then the going gets harder, through bracken and heather. After just over 1km the beck flows through a wood. The water flows steeply down rocks that can be scrambled up. More difficult ground has to be covered, but it becomes possible to use the stream bed in places. From time to time, you may see walkers, runners or cyclists on the bank above on the left. It is comforting to know that there is a path a short distance away on Mickleden Edge. At 193975 this path is only 100m away. But having got this far, continue up what is now named Bull Clough. The stream bed may be used for most of the next kilometre and height is gained gradually. There are a series of seemingly endless S-bends. Near the top, by a high peat bank, follow the left fork. When the clough eventually peters out at the top of the moor (185967) you are only 200m from the V1 crater (see Walk 22).

From here go west to the main path on the ridge. Take this south, over Cut Gate (the easy path you could have been on) to Margery Hill. You will pass a Bronze-Age barrow (mentioned in Walks 22 and 23). Margery Stones makes an ideal place to rest (2).

Now retrace your steps north along Howden Edge for nearly 2km to the trig. point at Outer Edge, passing near the wreckage of an Oxford aircraft (details in Walk 22). Continue for a further 1.5km, on a good path, with excellent all-round views.

Groughs are met above Harden Clough, and then at 172980 (17275/98023) a post, with the top painted red, marks the top of Near Cat Clough (3).

The short option is to follow a good path beside this clough, past grouse butts to The Porter (or Little Don River). The longer option is continue along Howden Edge, over Harden Moss and past Hoar

Stones for 2.5km to Loftshaw Clough Head (4). Turn north and take any clough, they all feed into Loftshaw Brook. Follow this down over difficult ground for 4km to where it becomes Horden Clough.

The two routes both lead to a footbridge at 174994 (5). From here, there is a path on the left bank of The Porter (or Little Don River). Look out for a fine sheep pen on the left. This is a pleasant way back to Langsett, and the car park. We found the party-goers by the bridge had been replaced by picnicking families.

# Section 5: Other Walks

This section contains two walks outside of the main areas and two long walks.

Combs Moss is now an open access area. Although it is on the White Peak district map, its terrain matches that of the Dark Peak rather than the limestone of the White Peak. The moor has a well-defined edge around its perimeter. The area south of Marsden, between the A635 and the A62, has a wide stretch of moorland and several reservoirs to explore.

One of the long walks is along the watershed of the River Etherow. This is partly on paths and partly over open moors. Some of the going underfoot is difficult. The other long walk is between Stockport and Sheffield. This is all on well-defined paths.

West Nab, trig. point to the right

# Walk 27. Combs Moss

**Grade:** Easy

**Distance:** 12km (7.5 miles)

**Time:** 3-5 hours

**Starting point/parking:** Lay-by for 3-4 cars, below Castle Naze, on the road from Combs (SK052786)

**Map:** OL 24

## General Description

The walk is on rough paths on the edge of the moor. This area has become open access with the 'right to roam' act. The walk goes past two of the points of Joe Brown's map reading/orienteering course (see the note at the end of this walk). On one corner there are the embankments of an Iron-Age hill fort. Below the edge are classic gritstone climbs. In clear weather there are excellent views along the entire walk.

Note: A sign by the stile near the start says dogs are not allowed.

## Route

From the lay-by go a few steps east, to a stile. On the way, look for one of Joe's points, on the wall on the left of the road. From the stile, ascend the hill past the open access sign. The outcrop at the top, Castle Naze, has several rock climbs, including one graded Very Severe called the Scoop. This is 30m right of the path that leads to the edge of the moor. At the top, turn left to go round the edge in a clockwise direction. Immediately the signs of the Iron Age hill fort are visible (1). There is a ditch across this north western corner that, together with the cliff on the west, and the steep slope to the north, appear to provide a small, defendable area. It is worthwhile inspecting the fort before continuing the walk.

Follow the edge in an easterly direction with, hopefully, fine views of the south side of Kinder Scout. After a 1km the edge swings south. A track goes east but keep to the high ground past Hob Tor. After another kilometer the trig point on Black Edge is reached (SK062770)

Chris Hill free-climbing The Scoop VS

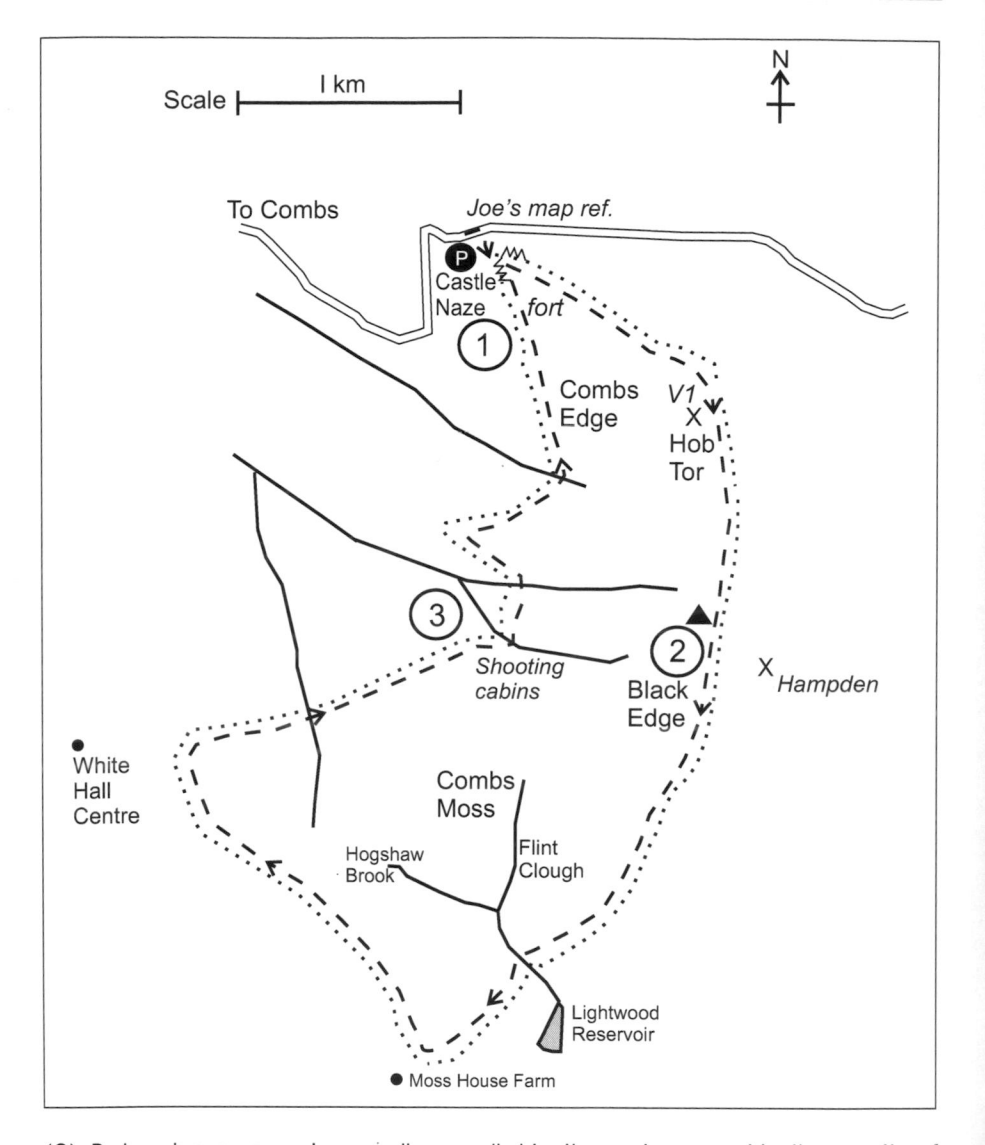

Scale ├──── I km ────┤

N

To Combs

*Joe's map ref.*

Castle Naze *fort*

(1)

Combs Edge

*V1*
X
Hob Tor

(2)

X *Hampden*

(3)

*Shooting cabins*

Black Edge

White Hall Centre

Combs Moss

Hogshaw Brook

Flint Clough

Lightwood Reservoir

● Moss House Farm

(2). Below here, over two walls parallel to the edge, and to the north of an east-west wall, there are a few bits of molten metal which are the remains of an aircraft wreck. Map ref: SK064768 (06390/76836). The airplane was a Hampden bomber.

Carry on along the edge for 2km to a gulley above Lightwood reservoir. This reservoir was empty, presumably for repair, on one occasion when we went past. We were impressed with the steepness of the sides and its depth. Turn west, and go round the top of the gulley. Then take the higher path that goes along the topside of a small, attractive wood. This takes you to the most southerly point of the plateau above Moss House Farm. Now, go NW, noting the old A6 coming up from Long Hill below. There are good views across to the ridge above Fernilee and Errwood reservoirs.

2km further along, the edge turns NE above the Whitehall Centre. The Centre is where Joe Brown worked when he designed the orienteering course. The cliffs and gulleys here are impressive and merit a closer look. The corner where the walk started may be seen in the far distance. However, the edge meanders for 4km on the way back. A locked shooting cabin, by another open stone hut is reached after walking along a muddy path (3). Another of Joe's instructions is in the vicinity of the huts.

From the cabin the track passes over two gulleys. Be careful to stay high, near the wall and not to follow the Land Rover track when it starts to descend from the edge. The path continues around a promontory back to the hill fort. Several times I have seen kestrels on this part of the edge. Once there were three of them, possibly a pair and their offspring

Note: I first came across Joe Brown's map reading trail in the Peak District Magazine (Feb 2001 issue). Sadly, I believe this fine magazine is no longer published. In the 1960s Joe worked as an instructor at the Whitehall Centre. Whilst there, he set up this trail by chiselling instructions into walls, bridges, gateposts etc. The instructions are either six-figure map reference numbers or a 3-figure bearing followed by the distance in yards. Each instruction leads you to the next point. The route is circular and may be started at any of the points.

Walk 33 is based on this course and gives further details.


Update:

Near Hob Tor there are small fragments by a pool that are possibly from a V1. Map ref: 061779 (06174/77901).

# Walk 28. West Nab, Wessenden Moor and Broadstone Hill

**Grade:** Strenuous

**Distance:** 17km (10.5 miles)

**Time:** 5-7 hours

**Starting point/parking:** Lay-by near junction of Wessenden Head Road and A635 Mossley to Holmfirth road (SE077076)

## General description

The walk goes west to Broadstone Hill. It goes to Diggle reservoir then back east to the Wessenden Reservoirs and West Nab. It is mainly off paths, along streams and over boggy moorland, to the north of the A635. An aircraft crash site is visited.

Although the distance isn't great it is difficult to make quick progress. I walked this alone in February on a day when the valleys never cleared of mist but above the mist it was calm and sunny.

## Route

From the car park take the path to Wessenden Head Reservoir. Cross the reservoir dam wall. On my walk in February, the mist was just spilling over the dam wall and the whole of the valley to the north was hidden by it. From the end of the dam a path curves west into Shiny Brook Clough (1). Follow this for 2km (don't take any of the left forks) to where it crosses the Pennine Way, 200m from the A635 (SE048066).

Carry on west for 1.5km over boggy ground, parallel to the road, to Hollin Brown Knoll. Keep on the high ground to Diggle Rake, with good views of the reservoirs to the south. Swing slightly north of west to the trig. point at Broadstone Hill (SE021069) (2). One summer, a short-eared owl flew out of a clough not far from the trig. point as I went past. On a clear day you should be able to see Diggle and its surrounding area. The plaque on the trig. point says that it was "cast down by vandals" and "rebuilt by Saddleworth Runners".

From the trig. point go 300m NE and find Wicken Clough. Follow this down to Diggle Reservoir (3). At SE024081 Wicken Clough meets South

Broadstone Hill

Clough, just above the reservoir. Return to this 'confluence' and go SE along the South Clough for 2 km. This stretch is enjoyable.

At SE039070 leave the clough and go 200m to the east to the P.W. (4). Cross it and take any of the many groughs that drain to the north. They all feed a stream which flows NE between Black Moss and White Moss. I presume a coin was used to allocate the two names. I once had to drag a friend out of a bog on White Moss. His white, cord trousers were never quite the same! This collection of cloughs develops into a nice stream that has two small waterfalls (SE050085). It is possible to descend both on the right-hand side. The first has a protruding finger of heather-covered rock that I managed to slide down by clinging to the heather. The second is mossy but there are good handholds on greasy rock.

Take the steps down to the stream that joins the two reservoirs (5). Cross this stream, turn right and follow the path on the north side of Wessenden Reservoir until it meets Sike Clough (SE063087). Go up this stream bed, over miniature waterfalls that, although mossy and muddy, are easily climbed. Follow the clough, keeping to the left when it forks, to the top of the ridge (SE067093).

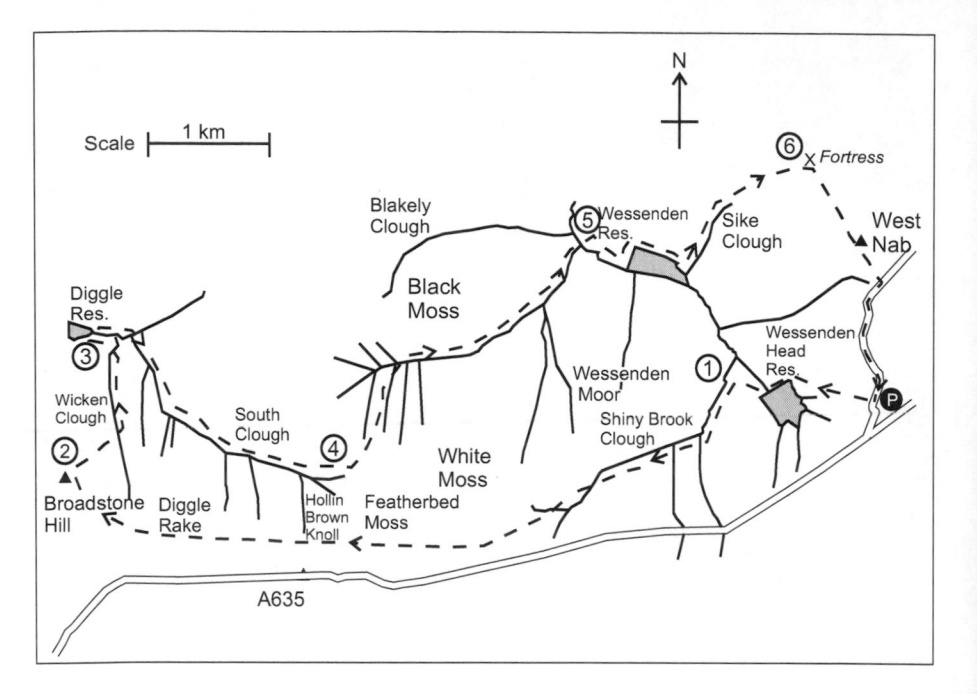

From the top, go 500m NE, to the site of wreckage from an American bomber, a B-17 Flying Fortress (6). Map ref: SE070095 (07084/09543). West Nab is 1km away, on a bearing of 150°. As I walked from the site of the B-17 to West Nab, late in the afternoon, the mist on each side of the ridge rose rapidly, leaving a narrow passage along the top. The mists quickly closed the gap and soon enveloped me. However, when I reached the trig. point at the top, I had climbed above the mist and there was a lovely view of the moors, with all the valleys hidden. From the trig. point go south to the minor road which leads back to the starting point.

# Walk 29. An Etherow Watershed

**Grade:** Very strenuous

**Distance:** 54km (34 miles)

**Time:** 13-17 hours

**Starting point/parking:** In Hollingworth, near The Organ (pub), either on Green Lane or in a car park by junction of Green Lane and A628 SK005963

## General description

The aim is to design a route to take in the main watershed of the River Etherow above Hollingworth. It is a long, arduous walk over difficult terrain and pathless in places. It is an excellent challenge, comparable to the Derwent Watershed.

My first attempt petered out in its early stages, when I lost time in cloud on Black Hill and having abandoned the idea, sat down and scoffed all my food supplies. I succeeded at my second attempt, by myself, in good conditions. This was in early summer in clear, cool weather. I set off at 7am, walking quickly with few stops, and finished at 6.30pm.

It is possible to shorten this walk by missing out the last part, by Cown Edge Rocks and Coombes Edge. This does not detract greatly from the walk (it doesn't shorten it by much either).

## Route

Opposite The Organ is Green Lane. Go up this, bending to the right after 400m. A further 300m brings you to Meadowbank Farm. Ignore Cow Lane, and take the second path, 20m further on. This is the Pennine Bridleway. Follow it round the farm. It is well marked and goes through Swallows Wood Reserve. At a junction, go straight on, round the right side of Lees Hill towards Swineshaw Reservoirs.

At SK011992 the path comes to a T-junction in front of an electricity pylon (1). Go under the pylon on a track across the top of Boar Flat, on a bearing of 030°. Cross a fence (there isn't a stile) and go north on the high part of the ridge. The hill in front rises to Hoarstone Edge. Try to judge which gulleys feed Higher Swineshaw Reservoir and which feed

Ogden Brook, and aim between them. The O.S. map marks an inspection chamber (SE014008). Pass by this, keeping north to Hoarstone Edge.

The Euro Constituency boundary line is followed for several miles, until well past Black Hill. From Hoarstone Edge go 120°, keeping on the highest ground. Cross a path by a cairn (SE026013), that goes to Chew Reservoir. Head 140° to Windgate Edge (SE032008), then east for 400m. Go 030° for 400m and then east for a further 800m to a trig. point at SE046012 (2). I got lost here on my first attempt.

From the trig. point go 060° to Laddow Moss, crossing a footpath (SE054016); then 040° for 400m past a cairn to a high point at SE056020. Now go 315° for 1 km across Black Chew Head (Greater Manchester's highest point). From here go 300m NE, then north, keeping Long Clough on your left. Go along Long Ridge over Howels Head. I once found a small thermometer here, just when I thought I might be the first person ever to stand in that particular bit of bog! Even after a dry spell this part was still wet.

At SE052038 swing to 060° for 500m to Round Hill, then north for 500m. Go east to Green Hill. At SE065046 head 130° until the Pennine Way is crossed. Now aim for the top of Black Hill, trying to judge the line, between the gulleys that forms the watershed.

I had my first rest at Black Hill trig. point (3), just before 11am, and met my first people of the walk. From the trig. point, go 070° past the gulley by Heyden Head. I dropped into the gulley to find the few remnants of a crashed Swordfish (SE083047). Back on the boundary follow the line towards the mast at Holme Moss.

Keep the mast on your left, and cross the A6024 by the car park. Take the path by the boundary fence to Britland Edge Hill (SE106026). Follow the fence past Withens Edge, to the trig. point at Dead Edge End (SE124017) (4). To keep exactly to the watershed you need to cross the fence and go east to Wike Head, judging the line between two groughs (SE135014), on a bearing of 110°. This line crosses above the Woodhead Tunnels near a pillar. Now turn south over Smallden Clough Head, dropping down to the main road near the junction with the minor road to Dunford Bridge. I stood at one point looking for this minor road, thinking that I was lost. However the road was hidden from view by the slope and was only l00m away.

From the junction, follow the main road east for a few metres, but you will see that the line of the watershed is to the right of the road, going up the middle of the hill to Lady Cross. This is 1km of awkward, tussocky grass. It is tempting to crack for the easy track just to the right. I reached Lady Cross at 1pm. The initials L.W.B. are etched on a stone.

From here (SK148998), go 210° to Round Hill. Continue on this bearing to Dean Head Stones (SK139982), though it is tempting to take the main path along Howden Edge. From Dean Head Stones go west and take the path that leads to Bleaklow Stones. This is a fairly true watershed between the River Etherow (flowing to the Irish Sea) and the River Derwent (flowing to the North Sea).

The path turns south at SK125980 then swings east again to Bleaklow Stones. It is marked by stakes and is fairly quick going. At one point, looking due north, I thought I could see Stoodley Pike. For those who've walked the Pennine Way, and read Barry Pilton's One Man and his Bog, remember that this can be the first sign of insanity! Now aim for Bleaklow Head (5). There are various paths and stakes but I still get lost on this section. Find the Wain Stones and head 200° towards Higher Shelf Stones. Then, near the extensive wreckage of a Superfortress, turn east towards Hern Clough. This drains towards the North Sea. Join the P.W. until it crosses the Snake Pass.

From here go 160° to Featherbed Moss summit (6), then turn west and rejoin the P.W. at SK083922. Follow the P.W. along the top of the watershed to Mill Hill. Take the path roughly west, past the wreckage of a Liberator. (More wreckage may be found further north of the path). Go over Burnt Hill and down to the A624 (7). You can follow this into Glossop, back to The Organ, and rightly feel well pleased with your efforts. However, I recommend a route that takes in more of the River Etherow's water collection area.)

Cross the A624 and take the Charlesworth road. After 1.5 km, at SK023912 take a track on the left to Higher Plainsteads Farm. Pass the farm on the right, go uphill and pass Rocks Farm on the right. Halfway along the building, take a path on the right and climb a stile. Keep Cown Edge Rocks on your left and, 400m from Rocks Farm, turn left across a field to Coombes Edge (8). Follow it as it curves to SK013925 (this is now the Pennine Bridleway). Turn right, and follow a track. This crosses a road, goes downhill to the north and reaches a junction (SK012932). Go straight across and down to Glossop Road. Turn right and after 500m go over a railway bridge.

The road bends to the right. Ignore the first signpost. Take the path 20m further on, signposted 'Trans Pennine Trail Longdendale'. This goes between houses to a road in Gamesley (9). Turn left and walk down the road, as it curves right, for 1km. Look for the sign 'Melandra Castle Ancient Monument'; this is the reason for coming this way. There is nothing left of the castle but one can imagine that this was a good site, overlooking the valley. Walk north, through the site, on mown

Plaque for Melandra Fort

grass. At the north corner, drop down, on one of the paths, to a road (which leads to the rubbish tip). Turn right to a footbridge over Glossop Brook at its confluence with the River Etherow. I've seen a kingfisher here. Go north to the main road to Glossop. Turn left to Woolley Bridge after 400m. Cross the river and take the footpath north, on the left bank. After 300m go through a gate and turn left up a lane. This passes the car park of The Organ. You may feel you deserve a quick half!

# Walk 30. Stockport to Sheffield

**Grade:** Very strenuous (but on good paths)

**Distance:** 56km (35 miles)

**Time:** 11-15 hours

**Starting point:** Stockport Town Hall

**Finishing point:** Sheffield Town Hall

## General description

A long walk, but mainly on paths, with some road work. The route could, obviously, be reversed depending on preference. We walked there and caught a late train back. An entertaining exercise would be to design an alternative route. Malcolm, Chris, Bob and I did this on a hot summer's day, a few years ago. We met at Stockport Town Hall at 7am. It was apparent that not all of us had had an early night.

## Route

Starting from the Town Hall, the first target is a footpath crossing the Stockport Golf Club course. Go south along the A6. After 1km, turn left down Nangreave Road. This becomes Hillcrest Road and leads to Marple Road (A626). Turn right towards Offerton Green. After 1.5 km take Shearwater Road on the right (1). Go past a mini roundabout and 80 yards after the junction with Grassholme Drive, take an alleyway on the left next to No. 25 Shearwater Road. This is a short cut to Offerton Road. Cross the road to a signpost marked Marple Mellor & Cown Edge. Take this path and cross Stockport Golf Course. After 600m a wood is reached. Go immediately through it and over Torkington Brook. 700m further, there is an old railway line, turn right along this for 250m. Then turn left, with trees on the left, by the edge of Marple Golf Course. After 750m there is a canal. Cross the canal bridge, which is just on the left, and take a lane (SE) for 200m to a road. Turn right, walk for l00m then go left, past a pub, The Crown. This is Hawk Green (2). At the end of this road, go straight across to a footpath that drops steeply down to a bridge over the Peak Forest canal. Go over the bridge and

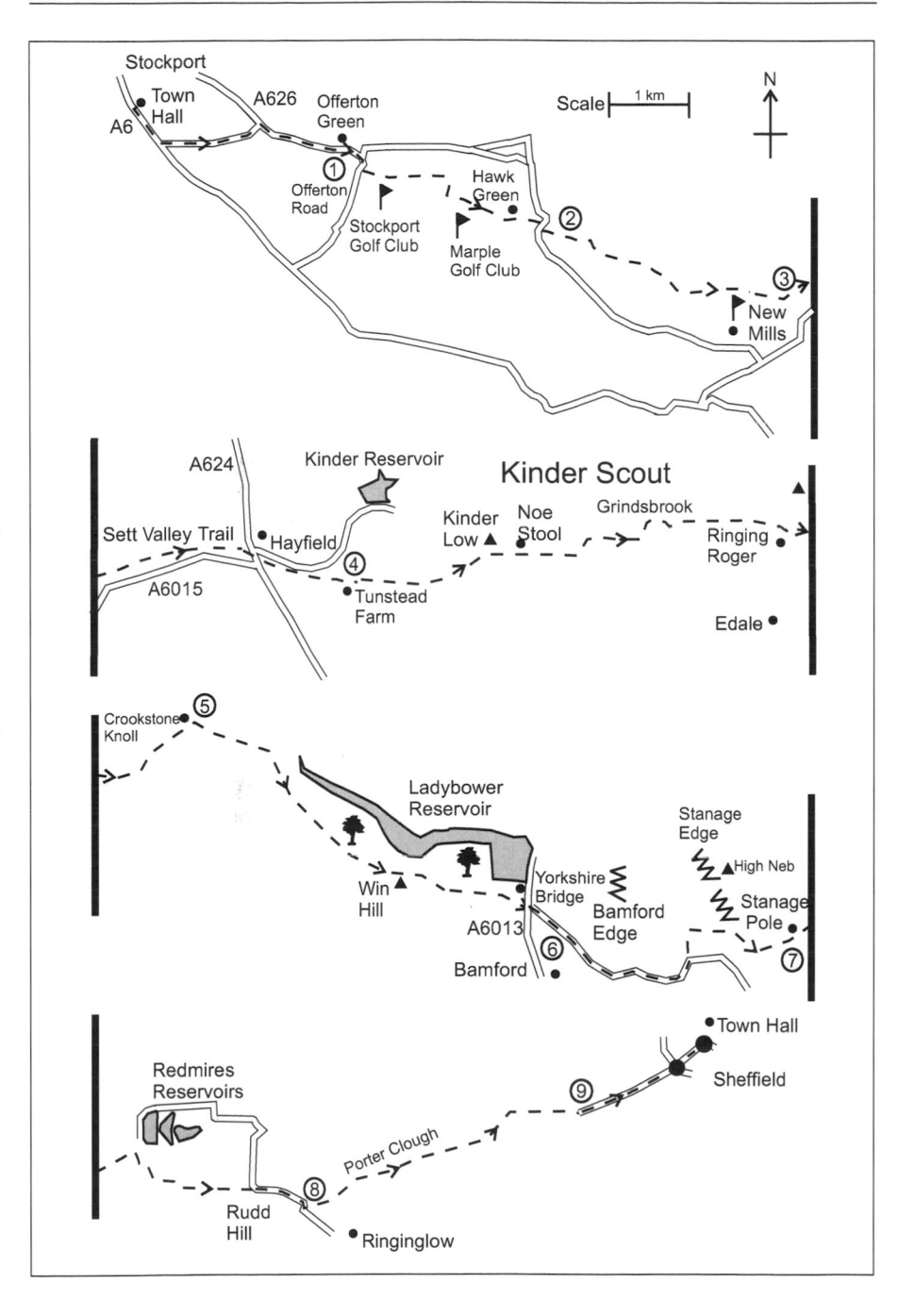

down to the New Mills road a few metres away. (The canal can be followed to New Mills but is a longer route).

Go south along this road and after about l00m, on the left, there is a signpost for a footpath (SK966874) that drops down to the River Goyt. (Note: For those wishing to avoid this complicated route the A626 and B6101, Marple-New Mills road, can be taken all the way from Stockport. We were trying to avoid roads as much as possible.)

An arched bridge is taken over the river. Turn right along the river. Then go under a railway bridge and along a track by the side of the line. Follow this track to Strines railway station. Take the path east (the Midshires Way). After 800m this leads to Brook Bottom Road. Turn right then, after 150m turn left. This track leads to New Mills Golf Course (SK994865). Continue east, straight on past the clubhouse and stay on the road down the hill, through a crossroads, for 1km until it joins a more major road. Turn right and after 200m turn left along a road that leads to the Sett Valley Trail (3). Walk down this trail into Hayfield. In the village, turn right, fork left and take the path along the south side of the River Kinder. Go past a campsite to Bowden Bridge. (There are Public Conveniences here). Turn right and then after 300m turn left to Tunstead Farm (4).

Go east uphill to Kinderlow End, pass to the south of the trig. point at Kinder Low and make for Noe Stool. Follow the path, east, along the edge to Crowden Tower. The path turns north past the top of Grindsbrook. It then swings east again past Upper Tor and Ringing Roger. Keep on the edge to Crookstone Out Moor. A path drops down from the far eastern corner of the plateau (SK143881) (5). Follow this path over Crookstone Hill, where it turns into a wider track. Take the path that loses the least height to Win Hill, and descend east, steeply downhill through the forest, to the River Derwent. Just over the bridge a path on the left leads to the road and Yorkshire Bridge.

We had planned to have a break in the Yorkshire Bridge Inn and also to meet two friends, Peter and Brian, who had caught a train to Bamford. They were to accompany us to Sheffield. These two left the pub first to get a head start.

From Yorkshire Bridge take the minor road (New Road) by a phone box (SK202849) which angles uphill below Bamford Edge (6). Walk along it for 3km. Then at SK225843, where the road turns right, go

Noe Stool

straight ahead following the track that climbs up to Stanage Edge. Go along the edge SE for 400m and take the track on the left to Stanage Pole (7).

Keep on the track until 200m from Redmires Reservoirs. Take a foot-path on the right that goes south of the reservoirs, over White Stones and by Rudd Hill, to Fulwood Road (SK277843).

On our trip we took a more direct route from Stanage Pole. We got lost, ended up at Ringinglow, and adjourned to the pub near the junction. Sitting comfortably in a corner were our missing comrades. They had also got lost and asked someone to point them towards Sheffield.

Go along Fulwood Lane for 1km and take the path on the left, along a small stream, Porter Clough (8). Follow this for nearly 5km to a roundabout (SK333856). Several roads are crossed but a pleasant route by various small lakes can easily be found. In Endcliffe Park there is a cairn and memorial plaque to the crew of an American B17 Flying Fortress that crashed nearby. At the roundabout take the main road (A625) into the centre of Sheffield (9). The roads are Ecclesall Road, straight on to Charter Row, right along Furnival Gate and left up Pinstone Street to the Town Hall. We retired to a nearby pub, The Globe, where not only were the customers friendly but so was the polecat that belonged to one of them.

We finished the walk at 8pm and this included stops for nearly two hours in pubs. Although the day was hot, the conditions were good. At the end of the evening, somewhat worse for wear, we caught the last train back to Stockport. It only took about an hour but we all fell asleep.

In 2004 Malc, Chris and myself attempted to reverse the walk, starting from Sheffield. Malc was taken ill near Edale, and escaped by train back to Stockport. In New Mills Chris complained about problems with his hip so we adjourned to a pub called the North Western, near one of the railway stations. After a couple of pints the momentum was lost so we rang Malc and asked him to come and collect us.

I think that a Stockport Sheffield route, or vice versa, would make a good annual charity walk.

# Further suggestions

These are some suggestions for walks that take in features that may not be visited on the listed walks. Only a brief outline of the route is given, as these are popular walks on paths that readers are likely to know.

The west face of Kinder in winter

# Walk 31. Kinder from Hayfield

**Distance:** 12km (7.5 miles)

**Starting point/parking:** Bowden Bridge (048869)

## Route:

Past Kinder Reservoir, up William Clough, along the western edge of the Kinder plateau, past Kinder Downfall, along to Kinder Low, and down to Tunstead Clough Farm.

This is a favourite walk that I never tire of. En route, the following items of interest may be seen.

Wreckage of a Sabre jet aircraft lies at the NW corner of the plateau. (Map Ref: SK069896 (06921/89643). See Walk 6.

About 800m from the NW corner, near the top of a path that makes a good short cut to the reservoir, there is a cross painted on a rock. Map Ref: SK072892 (07284/89210). See Walk 6.

Kinder Downfall is well known for the phenomenon of the water being blown upwards. There is a scramble up the waterfall that starts on the right and crosses through the fall to end up on the left. In good conditions it is rated as being moderately difficult.

600m after the top of Red Brook is crossed, there is a small amount of wreckage of a Hampden bomber. It is a few metres above the path, to the north of an outcrop that has a jagged edge. Map Ref: SK078874 (07806/87496). Recently a memorial plaque to the crew has been placed here.

The path from Kinder Low to Kinderlow End goes past a Bronze-Age barrow.

Just a few metres NE from the cairn on Kinderlow End there is a large patch of bare earth where a Miles Hawk crashed. Map Ref: SK073866 (07369/86698). There is no wreckage left but if you search you may find one or two tiny flakes of red or yellow paint. There is a small pile of stones at the side of the bare patch.

# Walk 32. Around the head of Edale

**Distance:** 15km (9.5 miles)

**Starting point/parking:** Barber Booth (107847)

### General description

There are several sites where aircraft crashed around Edale. A circuit of the top of the valley goes near these.

### Route:

From the bottom of Jacob's Ladder, climb up to the Woolpacks, walk to Edale Rocks, Brown Knoll, Lord's Seat and then cross the valley back towards Barber Booth.

250m below the Wool Packs, on a flat patch of land, there is a very small collection of wreckage from a Harvard aircraft. Map Ref: SK088868 (08891/86837). A further 200m or so south, there are two sites of wreckage from an Anson trainer. Map Ref: SK089867 (08905/86702) and an engine, in reeds, at SK088865 (08873/86579).

200m on a bearing of 300° from the trig. point at Brown Knoll leads to wreckage from an Oxford. Map ref: 081852 (08189/85202). See Walk 4.

A Thunderbolt crashed on Horsehead Tor. There is a cairn near the top of the gulley to the south of the Tor. The site of the wreckage is 100m, on a bearing of 070°, from the cairn at roughly the same height. Map ref: SK093843 (09356/84338). See Walk 4.

To the south of the ridge leading to Lord's Seat is small piece of molten metal from a Hampden aircraft. It is in a field high above a farm at SK104829 (10412/82994).

North of this ridge, near the very bottom of the slope, in a gulley, is part of the metal frame from another Oxford. This is best reached from the path that goes east from the bottom of Chapel Gate. It is 100m south of a wall at SK109838 (10949/83839).

# Walk 33. Joe Brown's map-reading course

**Distance: 32km (20 miles)**

**Start/finish:** Car park, The Street, above Errwood reservoir, (SK024752)

Joe Brown, the famous climber, devised this course while on the staff of the White Hall Outdoor Centre (see page 113). Some instructions have weathered but in most cases are not too difficult to find. For this reason it is advisable to break the course into sections. Without wanting to give too much away, I can say that the course takes in part of the Combs area (See Walk 27) and much of the Goyt Valley.

The instructions are two inches tall and are in relatively obvious places, such as at road junctions or under bridges. Remember there are two types of instructions (6-figure map reference and bearing/distance).

There are about twenty points over approximately 32km. One point was lost but has been replaced. This is at the little shrine by the side of the minor road that goes east from the Errwood and Fernilee reservoirs to the A5004 (old A6). This is a good place to start the trail. The shrine (map ref: 029753) has been rebuilt and Joe's instructions reinstated. The magazine article gave these as 188 284. This translates as 188 deg and 284 yards. This takes you to a nearby rise where there is a stone with the next instruction. (In fact, the article gave this as 188 x 284 deg. This led me to climb a wall topped by barbed wire and waste a considerable time wandering around in a nearby field!)

There is another point, not far from Errwood Hall, that I am unable to find. It may have been removed or it may be my incompetence. The magazine article did not say it was missing. In case you can't find it either, and to avoid your trail grinding to a halt, the missing numbers should be 007747. If you find the missing clue please let me know. This trail gave me several entertaining days out and eventually a group of us spent a day doing the entire route. My thanks to Joe and The Peak District magazine for the entertainment. At one point the trail even goes past a pub. It shows how thoughtful Joe was. Update: The missing clue has been found. The previous clue is inaccurate and should be 010741.

# Walk 34. The Two Inns Trail

**Grade:** No moderation

**Distance:** 1.5km (1 mile)

**Time:** Allow a minimum of 5 hours

**Starting and finishing point:** Edale railway station. There is a regular train service from Sheffield and Manchester.

## General description

This should be a short walk along good paths. The route is a 'there and back' walk. Do not underestimate the time required.

## Route

From the railway station walk along the approach, to the road that leads to Edale. Turn left and after 100m enter The Rambler. Take refreshment here. When ready, leave and return to the road. Turn left

The Old Nag's Head

and after 600m look out for The Old Nags Head. Go inside, where further refreshments are available. After a suitable period, exit carefully from the building and retrace your steps for 600m (or more) to The Rambler. Remember the time of your train home and return to the Edale railway station. In poor conditions, allow plenty of time and make sure you wait on the correct platform.

# Appendix: Aircraft wrecks

The table below lists all the crash sites I have found. It may not be a complete list of all the sites in the Dark Peak but it contains most of them.

I have used a GPS to record the map references. In many cases there is very little wreckage and the usual six-figure reference is not accurate enough to locate the site easily. Hence, I have given the GPS ten figure reference. This should lead you to within 10 metres or so of the site. For example, from the first line of the table: 11091/86014. The 11091 is the easting and 86014 the northing. The equivalent 6-fig. ref. would be 110860. This would give a 100m square to search.

All but one of the following sites are on the Ordnance Survey Dark Peak OL1 Explorer map. Amount of wreckage: L – large; M – medium; S – small; E – extremely small; O – no wreckage, just a crater

| Aircraft | Date | Place | 10-fig map ref | Size | Walk |
|---|---|---|---|---|---|
| Heyford K6875 | 22/07/37 | Grindslow Knoll | SK11091/86014 | S | 3 |
| Blenheim L1476 | 30/01/39 | Torside | SK08304/97008 | S | 8 |
| Swordfish P4223 | 25/01/40 | Black Hill | SE08343/04768 | S | 16/29 |
| Hampden L4055 | 23/05/40 | Holme | SE09919/05751 | O | 16 |
| Hampden | 30/09/40 | Combes Moss | SK06390/76836 | E | 27 |
| Hampden X3154 | 21/12/40 | Rushup Edge | SK10412/82994 | E | 32 |
| Defiant N1766 | 12/04/41 | Rowlee Pasture | SK15459/90482 | S | 14 |
| Wellington W5719 | 31/07/41 | Upper Tor, Edale | SK11061/87535 | S | 2 |
| Lysander V9403 | 19/08/41 | Chew Res. | SE04069/03245 | S | 15 |
| Defiant | 29/08/41 | Bleaklow Stones | SK10613/96934 | S | 10 |
| Botha W5103 | 10/12/41 | Bleaklow | SK11095/97524 | M | 10 |
| Hampden AE381 | 21/01/42 | Kinder | SK07806/87496 | S | 31 |
| Wellington DV810 | 09/12/42 | Broomhead Moor | SK23482/95419 | S | 24 |
| Wellington X3348 | 26/01/43 | Blackden Edge | SK12805/87556 | S | 2 |
| Wellington R1011 | 30/01/43 | Birchen Bank | SK10544/98578 | S | 9/10 |
| Thunderbolt P47 | 25/04/43 | Horsehill Tor, Edale | SK09356/84338 | S | 4/32 |
| Halifax HR727 | 05/10/43 | Blackden Edge | SK13101/87634 | S | 2 |
| Oxford LX518 | 19/10/43 | Margery Hill | SK18025/96710 | S | 22/26 |
| Liberator PB4Y | 18/12/43 | Broken Ground | SE00875/01203 | S | 21 |
| Lightning P38J | 10/05/44 | Tintwistle | SK03926/99084 | S | 21 |
| Stirling LJ628 | 21/07/44 | Margery Hill | SK20157/95524 | L | 22/23 |
| Liberator B-24H-20 | 09/10/44 | Holme Moss | SE10639/03374 | S | 16 |
| Liberator B-24J | 11/10/44 | Burnt Hill, Mill Hill | SK05733/90597 | M | 6/29 |
| Mosquito PF395 | 22/10/44 | Dovestone Res. | SE02569/03184 | S | 15 |
| V1 Fieseler 103 | 24/10/44 | Margery Hill | SK16566/96507 | O | 22/26 |
| Anson N9912 | 11/12/44 | Edale | SK10112/87861 | S | 3 |

| Hurricanes PZ851, | | | | | |
|---|---|---|---|---|---|
| 765 + 854 | 22/02/45 | Tintwistle | SK03562/98890 | E | 21 |
| Oxford NM683 | 04/03/45 | Rushup Edge | SK10949/83839 | S | 32 |
| Fortress B-17G-65 | 06/04/45 | Wessenden | SE07084/09543 | M | 28 |
| Tiger Moth T6164 | 12/04/45 | Chew Res. | SE03353/01585 | S | 15/21 |
| Lancaster KB993 | 18/05/45 | James Thorn | SK07921/94784 | S | 7 |
| C-47 Skytrain | 24/07/45 | James Thorn | SK08051/94733 | M | 7 |
| Anson NL185 | 23/11/45 | Woolpacks | SK08873/86579 | S | 32 |
| Oxford HN594 | 28/12/45 | Brown Knoll | SK08189/85202 | M | 4/32 |
| Superfortress RB-29A | 03/11/48 | Higher Shelf Stones | SK09066/94878 | L | 7/11 |
| Lancaster PA411 | 20/12/48 | Tintwistle | SK03563/99263 | S | 21 |
| Dakota G-AHCY | 19/08/49 | Wimberry Stones | SE01491/02669 | S | 15 |
| Meteor RA487 | 08/12/50 | Haggside, Derwent | SK16592/89027 | S | 14 |
| Meteors WA971, | | | | | |
| VZ518 | 12/04/51 | Sliddens Moss | SE06853/02859 | L | 17/20 |
| Consul TF-RPM | 12/04/51 | Margery Hill | SK17407/96628 | M | 22 |
| Chipmunk WB579 | 03/07/51 | Arnfield Res. | SK02733/99872 | S | |
| Harvard FT415 | 14/01/52 | Woolpacks | SK08891/86837 | S | 32 |
| Sabres XD707 | | | SK06921/89643+ | M | |
| XD730 | 22/07/54 | Ashop Edge | SK07280/90226 | M | 5/6/31 |
| Sabre F86E | 14/12/54 | Black Hill | SE09100/05070 | M | 16 |
| Beaver L-20A5 | 05/12/56 | Bramah Edge | SK05533/97592 | S | |
| Miles Hawk G-AJSF | 29/07/57 | Kinder Low | SK07369/86698 | E | 31 |
| Dragon Rapide | 30/12/63 | Kinder | SK10159/88242 | S | 3 |
| **Updates:** | | | | | |
| Hunter XL595 | 11/06/93 | Dukes Road | SK 20851/94345 | M | 24 |
| Vampire WA400 | 25/07/51 | Strines Moor | SK 21844/89801 | S | |
| V1 | 27/12/44 | Combs Moss | SK 06174/77901 | S | 27 |
| Wellington Z8980 | 17/07/42 | Stanedge | SK 26157/83824 | M | 25 |

The Shining Tor sites, listed below, and the Combs Moss site, above, are on the White Peak OL24 map. The following sites are on Shining Tor, near Errwood Reservoir.

| Defiant | 16/10/41 | Shining Tor | SJ99838/73569 | E |
|---|---|---|---|---|
| Oxford LX745 | 12/03/44 | Shining Tor | SJ99829/74664 | S |
| Harvard | 30/11/44 | Shining Tor | SJ99749/73746 | E |

For further information about these crashes I recommend Ron Collier's books Dark Peak Aircraft Wrecks 1 & 2. There are helpful web sites on the internet, in particular Alan Clark's site: www.peakdistrictaircrashes.co.uk

Insert Dark Peak Hikes Doug Brown in Google to find website with more photographs of the routes and further information on Dark Peak Hikes & Lakeland Hikes. The website also includes information about letterboxes in the Dark Peak District and Lakeland.

# Also of Interest

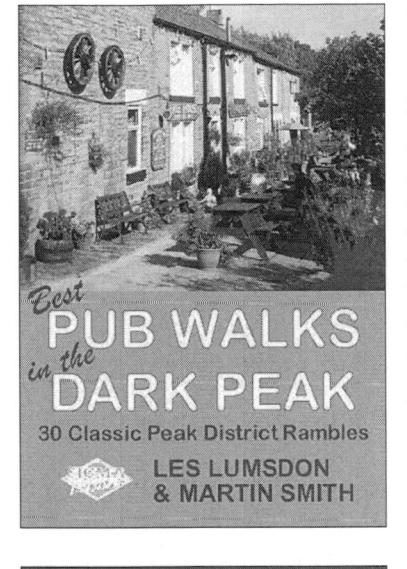

## BEST PUB WALKS IN THE DARK PEAK

*Les Lumsdon and Martin Smith*

This is a completely revised and updated edition of one of Sigma's best-selling and authoritative walking guides. The companion volume to 'Best Pub Walks in the White Peak', this guide concentrates on the high ground of the northern Peak District.

The 30 rambles range from 3 to 11 miles and all start or call at one of the many Peakland pubs in and around the picturesque villages such as Rainow in the west, Castleton and Glossop in the north, and Baslow in the east. £7.95

## WALKS IN THE ANCIENT PEAK DISTRICT 2nd Edition

*Bob Harris*

This collection of walks visits the prehistoric monuments and sites of the Peak District, including the White Peak, Dark Peak, Western and Eastern Moors. Explore rock shelters and caves of the old stone age, stone circles and burial chambers of the Neolithic and Bronze Ages and the great hill forts of the Iron Age, while appreciating the beautiful scenery and wildlife of the Peak District.

Not only a book of walks but also a refreshing insight into life during these early times, including the thinking behind the monuments, rituals and strange behaviour of our ancestors! £8.99

## PEAK DISTRICT NATURAL HISTORY WALKS 2nd Edition

*Chris Mitchell*

A practical guide featuring 18 walks exploring the living landscape of this beautiful area, following on from the very successful edition for the Lake District by the same author. Presented in an accessible and entertaining form the case notes will appeal equally to families, ramblers, or hill walkers of all ages whose eyes will be trained to see the unexpected. It also offers much to those wishing a more educational or academic slant, wildlife enthusiasts, teachers and field-study leaders. *£8.99*

## LAKELAND HIKES
## Off the Beaten Track

*Doug Brown*

30 walks in one of the most beautiful regions of Great Britain, renowned for its fell walking and landscape of lakes, tarns, rivers, valleys, cliffs, ridges and mountain peaks. Explore the hidden Lakeland and discover the remoter areas and lesser-used routes up the main peaks; visit out-of-the-way gills and crags.

Test your navigational skills by locating aircraft wrecks, old memorials, fill forts, a stone circle, classic rock climbs, caves, mines, and remnants of an industrial past.
£7.95

All of our books are all available on-line or through booksellers. For a free catalogue, please contact: Sigma Leisure, Stobart House, Pontyclerc, Penybanc Road, Ammanford, Carmarthenshire SA18 3HP

Tel: 01269 593100   Fax: 01269 596116

**info@sigmapress.co.uk      www.sigmapress.co.uk**